OLD TESTAMENT MESSAGE

A Biblical-Theological Commentary

Carroll Stuhlmueller, C.P. and Martin McNamara, M.S.C.

EDITORS

Old Testament Message, Volume 5

Joshua, Judges
with an
Excursus on Charismatic
Leadership in Israel

Leslie Hoppe, O.F.M.

Michael Glazier, Inc.
Wilmington, Delaware

First published in 1982 by: MICHAEL GLAZIER, INC., 1723 Delaware Avenue, Wilmington, Delaware 19806
Distributed outside U.S., Canada & Philippines by: GILL & MACMILLAN, LTD., Goldenbridge, Inchicore, Dublin 8 Ireland

Library of Congress Catalog Card Number: 82-83724
International Standard Book Number
  Old Testament Message series: 0-89453-235-9
  JOSHUA-JUDGES
    0-89453-240-5 (Michael Glazier, Inc.)
    7171-1169-5 (Gill & Macmillan, Ltd.)

Cover design by Lillian Brulc
Cartography by Lucille Dragovan
Typography by Susan Pickett

Printed in the United States of America

*To the Friars of the Assumption
Province Order of Friars Minor*

Table of Contents

The Book of Judges

Maps

Editors' Preface

Old Testament Message brings into our life and religion today the ancient word of God to Israel. This word, according to the book of the prophet Isaiah, had soaked the earth like "rain and snow coming gently down from heaven" and had returned to God fruitfully in all forms of human life (Isa 55:10). The authors of this series remain true to this ancient Israelite heritage and draw us into the home, the temple and the market place of God's chosen people. Although they rely upon the tools of modern scholarship to uncover the distant places and culture of the biblical world, yet they also refocus these insights in a language clear and understandable for any interested reader today. They enable us, even if this be our first acquaintance with the Old Testament, to become sister and brother, or at least good neighbor, to our religious ancestors. In this way we begin to hear God's word ever more forcefully in our own times and across our world, within our prayer and worship, in our secular needs and perplexing problems.

Because life is complex and our world includes, at times in a single large city, vastly different styles of living, we have much to learn from the Israelite Scriptures. The Old Testament spans forty-six biblical books and almost nineteen hundred years of life. It extends through desert, agricultural and urban ways of human existence. The literary style embraces a world of literature and human emotions. Its history began with Moses and the birth-pangs of a new people, it came of an age politically and economically under David and Solomon, it reeled under the fiery threats of prophets like Amos and Jeremiah. The people despaired and yet were re-created with new hope during the Babylonian exile. Later reconstruction in the homeland and then the trauma of apocalyptic movements prepared for the revelation of "the mystery hidden for ages in God who created all things" (Eph 3:9).

While the Old Testament telescopes twelve to nineteen hundred years of human existence within the small country of Israel, any single moment of time today witnesses to the reenactment of this entire history across the wide expanse of planet earth. Each verse of the Old Testament is being relived somewhere in our world today. We need, therefore, the *entire* Old Testament and all twenty-three volumes of this new set, in order to be totally a "Bible person" within today's widely diverse society.

The subtitle of this series—"A Biblical-Theological Commentary"—clarifies what these twenty-three volumes intend to do.

Their *purpose* is theological: to feel the pulse of God's word for its *religious* impact and direction.

Their *method* is biblical: to establish the scriptural word firmly within the life and culture of ancient Israel.

Their *style* is commentary: not to explain verse by verse but to follow a presentation of the message that is easily understandable to any serious reader, even if this person is untrained in ancient history and biblical languages.

Old Testament Message—like its predecessor, *New Testament Message*—is aimed at the entire English-speaking world and so is a collaborative effort of an international team. The twenty-one contributors are women and men drawn from North America, Ireland, Britain and Australia. They are scholars who have published in scientific journals, but they have been chosen equally as well for their proven ability to communicate on a popular level. This twenty-three book set comes from Roman Catholic writers, yet, like the Bible itself, it reaches beyond interpretations restricted to an individual church and so enables men and women rooted in biblical faith to unite and so to appreciate their own traditions more fully and more adequately.

Most of all, through the word of God, we seek the blessedness and joy of those

who walk in the law of the Lord!...

who seek God with their whole heart (Ps. 119:1-2).

Carroll Stuhlmueller, C.P.   Martin McNamara, M.S.C.

Introduction

The Deuteronomic History

While the Books of Joshua and Judges are sometimes treated as individual literary works, they are merely components of a larger literary unit which rabbinic tradition has named "the Former Prophets." Besides Joshua and Judges, the Former Prophets include the Books of Samuel and Kings. These books were considered to be part of the prophetic corpus because the ancient rabbis believed that prophets were responsible for their composition: Joshua (the Book of Joshua), Samuel (the Books of Judges and Samuel) and Jeremiah (the Book of Kings).

Like the rabbis of antiquity, modern Biblical scholarship sees the Books of Joshua to 2nd Kings as forming a literary unit. It has been suggested that Joshua, Judges, Samuel and Kings were originally composed during the Exile (c. 550 B.C.) to explain the destruction of the Temple, the loss of the land and the tragedy of the Exile itself. The theological views which served to provide the explanation for these disasters were taken from the Book of Deuteronomy. This latter book became the introduction to the history of Israel in her land from the time of her settlement in it (Joshua) to her dispossession from it (2 Kings). In view of its dependence upon Deuteronomy's theological perspectives, the entire literary complex running from Joshua to 2nd Kings with its introduction (Deuteronomy) has been called the Deuteronomistic History of Israel (DtrH).

As is usually the case with scholarly hypotheses, the one concerning DtrH has engendered much additional study. Over the years there have been a number of suggestions to modify the hypothesis described above. One alternative suggests that the bulk of DtrH was written during the reign of King Josiah of Judah (640-609 B.C.) to bolster his supposed reforms (*cf.,* 2 Kgs 22-23). A second definitive edition was made during the Exile (587-539 B.C.) to explain the failure of this reform and the fall of Jerusalem that followed a few years later.

A more recent alternative posits three editions of DtrH. The first is one which is positively oriented to the Davidic dynasty and sees Judah's future as wedded to that of the dynasty. A second edition was made to highlight the role of the monarchy's great antagonists: the prophets. Israel's troubles are explained as due to her failure to heed the prophets sent to her. Hope for the future lies in a determination to heed the prophets sent by the Lord. A third and final edition was prompted by the publication of the Book of Deuteronomy. The book guaranteed a future for Israel if she obeyed the Law. Disobedience has brought nothing but disaster.

Study of the literary history of DtrH will go on. In this commentary the primary focus will be on the final form of DtrH, the stage which all admit was greatly influenced by Deuteronomic perspectives. When this commentary speaks of the "Deuteronomist," it refers to the author of the final and definitive edition of the Deuteronomistic History.

Holy War

One problem faced by contemporary readers of Joshua and Judges is the attitude of these books towards the wars of conquest which they describe as the means by which Israel acquired the land which was to be the scene of her subsequent history. This attitude is derived from the Holy War ideology of Deuteronomy (*cf.,* Deut 20:1-20). The term

"Holy War" is certainly an infelicitous expression (it does not occur in the Bible), yet it has been coined to describe the Israelite belief which holds that it was God who fought the battles against Israel's enemies. The land then was not acquired by Israel's military prowess but was received as a gift from God.

From a historical perspective, Deuteronomy's Holy War ideology was just that—ideology. It is very doubtful that Holy War was anything more than a vehicle for ancient Israel's confession of faith in her Lord. In other words, the descriptions of the battles in Joshua and Judges are more ideological statements than historical reports. There have been attempts to diminish the harshness of those battle reports. For example, it has been suggested that the Hebrew word which is usually translated as "thousand" actually referred to the village muster which hardly ever numbered above 20. The numbers of those who fought and died in the wars of conquest then must be revised downward. Similarly some consider the *herem* (the massacre of all enemy people by the victorious army) to have been a measure to control plague so that the impetus for the *herem* comes not from ferocity but from hygiene. Similarly the wars of conquest have been described as social revolutionary movements which aimed to overthrow the harsh and oppressive leadership classes of a number of Canaanite city-states. The worshippers of Yahweh who escaped from Egypt became the catalyst for these revolutions since they proved that it was indeed possible to be victorious in the face of seemingly insurmountable odds. Eventually these successful revolutions came to be seen as the victories of Yahweh who takes the side of the oppressed. Finally it should be noted that sometimes the acquisition of territory took place peacefully. For example, the city of Shechem apparently entered the Israelite coalition without any violent confrontations.

While these attempts to explain the apparent harshness of the Holy War as a misunderstanding of the actual historical circumstances may be quite convincing, they cannot entirely eliminate the fact that ancient Israel did acquire the land, in part, through violent means. While this may offend our sensibilities today, that fact cannot be ignored without ignoring the bulk of Joshua and Judges. The question then shifts: how can this violence be justified theologically? The ideology of Holy War is not any more difficult to explain than the necessity of Jesus' death. Both are attempts to describe the mysterious ways by which God uses human folly and sin as a means of salvation. The basic message of the entire Bible is summed up in Joseph's response to his brothers who feared his retribution for their crime against him: "As for you, you meant evil against me; but God meant it for good, to bring it about that many people should be kept alive, as they are today" (Gen 50:20). The wars that took place during the settlement period were evil—there is no denying that. (The identity and culpability of human agents responsible for that evil is another question.) What the Bible does affirm is that God's purpose was served even by this evil.

Admittedly reading some episodes of ancient Israel's early history in her land does not make for pleasant reading. History is hardly ever edifying. Even the history of the early Church had its dark moments (*cf.,* Acts 5:1-11). DtrH was not written to edify but to shock Judah into obedience. The Deuteronomists were hoping against hope that the disaster they had experienced and were trying to explain to their readers was not the end of the story. Their faith in the God who brings good out of human sin remained constant. It is that faith which gave rise to DtrH.

Archaeology

It has been just a little less than one hundred years since archaeologists have begun systematic excavations in the territory occupied by ancient Israel. It was hoped that their work would clear up some of the problems in reconstructing the history of the settlement period. The Bible, after all, does not give an entirely coherent picture of ancient Israel's first occupation of the land. The Book of Joshua gives the impression that this occupation was accomplished with quick and decisive military campaigns by the united tribal armies of Israel under the leadership of Joshua. These victories involved the total subjugation if not annihilation of the indigenous population of Canaan. On the other hand, the Book of Judges shows that the Canaanites caused continuing problems for Israel and that the occupation of the land was a gradual process which took place over a very long period of time. Any military action that took place was the act of individual tribes and clans or, at best, of small coalitions of tribes which were led by a number of individuals.

While expectations regarding the outcome of archaeological excavations in Palestine were high, the results of the excavations have complicated the picture of the settlement period even more. For example, archaeologists have shown that a number of sites (*e.g.,* Dan, Bethel and Hazor) do show destruction levels that could be attributed to the Israelite incursion into Palestine. In contrast, there is no archaeological evidence that Jericho, Ai and Gibeon were destroyed or even occupied during the settlement period. Not only has archaeology been unable to clarify the history of this period, it has provided us with new problems.

One of the greatest shortcomings of Palestinian archaeology is that for the most part it is "silent," *i.e.,* precious little written materials have been found in the course of excavations. (Qumran is a notable exception to this general situation.) When excavating a site from the Biblical period, archaeologists consider themselves extremely fortunate when they find a broken potsherd with some distinct lettering on it. Most often the Bible provides the framework for the archaeologist's interpretation of the material uncovered in the process of excavation. Since the site provides no written materials to aid in understanding its culture, recourse is made to the Biblical text. Any attempt to use this data to support the historicity of the Biblical narrative then is an exercise in circular reasoning. Those who try to use archaeology to "prove" the historical value of the Bible do nothing more than prove their own interpretation of the Bible—an interpretation made, most often, long before the archaeologist's spade was thrust into the earth.

What archaeology can do for serious students of the Bible is the re-creation of the temporal and spatial context which provided the physical environment for the people and events mentioned in the Bible. Excavation can reveal the quality of that environment's economic, social and political system. It can even describe those people's diet, occupations and aesthetic sense. In terms of confirming the historicity of the Bible, however, archaeology has proven to be ambiguous at best.

At the present time, some Palestinian archaeologists are suggesting that their science undergo a profound shift in emphasis in order to find its own identity as a discipline apart from its relationship to Biblical studies or even history. The result of this shift in emphasis has been a concern for the development of a refined method of field archaeology and the widening of the scope of material gathered. The result of this growing sophistication is a more comprehensive view of each site's material culture and a more careful chronology of each site. In addition, with this development there has come a flood of information which the interpreter of the Bible must take into account, but such data can be employed effectively only if the interpreter understands what archaeology can and cannot do.

The Theology of Joshua and Judges

While this commentary does focus on the theological perspectives of the final form of Joshua and Judges, it does attempt to take into account the religious concerns of the earlier forms of this material. For example, some texts do display an earlier etiological interest, *i.e.,* a concern to explain the origin of a particular monument or settlement. Such interest will be noted at relevant points in the text. The diverse earlier material found in Joshua and Judges has

been preserved because it was used as a vehicle to describe
what happened to Israel and Judah at a much later date.
These books really try to explain why the land of promise
was lost and why that nation freed by God from slavery in
Egypt now faced exile in Babylon. Joshua and Judges provide the first chapters of DtrH. Already we find the self-
destructive tendencies of Israel. What began with such
promise in Joshua ends with almost total chaos in Judges.
The goal of the final form of the history of Israel in her land
was quite simple: to encourage the Chosen People of God to
choose the way of obedience. Fidelity to the law of God is
the only hope for any future in the land: "If you obey the
commandments of the Lord your God...the Lord your
God will bless you in the land....But if your heart turns
away...you shall not live long in the land..."(Deut 30:16-
18).

How To Use This Commentary

One of the most helpful insights of recent Biblical scholarship has been the recognition that the Books of Joshua and
Judges are part of a larger literary complex known as the
Deuteronomistic History. One consequence of this insight
should be the readers' determination to become familiar
with this literary unit as a whole rather than piecemeal. The
goal of this commentary is to help the readers begin working
through the first components of the Deuteronomistic History: Joshua and Judges. The best way to use this book is to
read through it in its entirety rather than to use it as a
reference tool in order to prepare a Bible study or a sermon
on a specific passage. Only when readers become familiar
with Joshua and Judges as a large unit can they use the
commentary on individual sections with profit and understanding.

This commentary focuses on the theological concerns of
the Books of Joshua and Judges. While the historical and
literary dimensions are not ignored, they are discussed in

such a way as to illuminate the religious perspectives of the Deuteronomists. The literary artistry of Joshua and Judges as well as their historical value cannot be underestimated. Yet the Deuteronomists composed these texts as a confession of faith in the Lord. They have been treasured by the Synagogue and the Church as religious documents and so they ought to be read and appreciated by believers today.

THE BOOK OF JOSHUA

THE BOOK OF JOSHUA

The Deuteronomistic Introduction
1:1-18

The first chapter of Joshua is similar in structure to the
Book of Deuteronomy in which four titles (Deut 1:1; 4:44;
29:1; 33:1) introduce the words of Moses. Here four verses
(vv. 1, 10, 12, 16a) provide a narrative framework for the
four speeches which are the heart of Josh 1: the Lord's
speech to Joshua (vv. 1-9), Joshua's speech to his officers
(vv. 10-11), Joshua's speech to the Transjordan tribes (vv.
12-15) and their reply (vv. 16-18). No action or movement is
described in these speeches; they serve to introduce the
reader to the theological perspectives from which the "conquest" will be interpreted.

THE LORD'S SPEECH TO JOSHUA
1:1-9

1 After the death of Moses the servant of the Lord, the
Lord said to Joshua the son of Nun, Moses' minister,
²"Moses my servant is dead; now therefore arise, go over
this Jordan, you and all this people, into the land which I
am giving to them, to the people of Israel. ³Every place
that the sole of your foot will tread upon I have given to
you, as I promised to Moses. ⁴From the wilderness and

this Lebanon as far as the great river, the river Euphrates, all the land of the Hittites to the Great Sea toward the going down of the sun shall be your territory. ⁵No man shall be able to stand before you all the days of your life; as I was with Moses, so I will be with you; I will not fail you or forsake you. ⁶Be strong and of good courage; for you shall cause this people to inherit the land which I swore to their fathers to give them. ⁷Only be strong and very courageous, being careful to do according to all the law which Moses my servant commanded you; turn not from it to the right hand or to the left, that you may have good success wherever you go. ⁸This book of the law shall not depart out of your mouth, but you shall mediate on it day and night, that you may be careful to do according to all that is written in it; for then you shall make your way prosperous, and then you shall have good success. ⁹Have I not commanded you? Be strong and of good courage; be not frightened, neither be dismayed; for the Lord your God is with you wherever you go."

The focus here is on the impending fulfillment of the promises made to the patriarchs (v. 6). Under the leadership of Joshua, Israel will soon come to possess the land of promise (*cf.,* Deut 1:8). Obedience to "the book of the law" is the only requirement for the success of the project which Joshua and the Israelites are about to undertake. Questions of military strategy do not even need to be considered.

The content and phraseology of this speech are strongly reminiscent of Deuteronomy. For example, vv. 4-5 are an expansion of Deut 11:24f. Verses 6-9 are a montage of Deuteronomic texts and expressions (*cf.,* Deut 3:28; 5:29; 7:21; 17:19; 24:8; 31:9). Most noteworthy of all is the emphasis on obedience to the divine will as written in "the book of the law" (v. 8), *i.e.,* Deuteronomy (*cf.,* Deut 28:58; 31:10; 6:6f).

The boundaries of the promised land given in v. 4 are broader than those which ancient Israel ever achieved in fact. This joined with the assurances of success (vv. 5, 7, 9) is poignantly significant given the situation which obtained when these words were written. The land of promise was partially abandoned by Israel. It was completely absorbed into a foreign empire. The inheritors of the promise were dispersed and in exile. Certainly the admonition in v. 9b is a remarkable product of faith in the God of the promise.

JOSHUA'S SPEECH TO HIS OFFICERS
1:10-11

> [10]Then Joshua commanded the officers of the people, [11]"Pass through the camp, and command the people, 'Prepare your provisions; for within three days you are to pass over this Jordan to go in to take possession of the land which the Lord your God gives you to possess.'"

After receiving his orders from the Lord, Joshua passes these on to the leaders of the people. The impression left by Joshua's words is that Israel's entrance into the land will be peaceful. Since Israel's possession of the land has been decreed by the Lord, it will take place. The people simply have to gather provisions for their journey into the land.

JOSHUA'S SPEECH TO THE TRANSJORDAN TRIBES
1:12-15

> [12]And to the Reubenites, the Gadites, and the half-tribe of Manasseh Joshua said, [13]"Remember the word which Moses the servant of the Lord commanded you, saying, 'The Lord your God is providing you a place of rest, and will give you this land.' [14]Your wives, your little ones, and your cattle shall remain in the land which Moses gave you beyond the Jordan; but all the men of valor among you shall pass over armed before your brethren and shall help them, [15]until the Lord gives rest to your brethren as well

> as to you, and they also take possession of the land which the Lord your God is giving them; then you shall return to the land of your possession, and shall possess it, the land which Moses the servant of the Lord gave you beyond the Jordan toward the sunrise."

Here the acquisition of the land is clearly a military undertaking which will involve all the tribes including those which have already acquired their allotments in Transjordan (*cf.,* Num 32; Deut 3:18-20). Once this operation is completed, all the tribes will be able to enjoy the "rest" which the Lord will give Israel (vv. 13, 15). In the Deuteronomic tradition, this rest surrounds Israel with security and peace, God's gift for obedience to the divine will (Deut 3:20; 12:10; 25:19; Josh 21:44; 22:4; 23:1; Judg 3:11, 30; 1 Kgs 5:4).

THE REPLY OF THE TRANSJORDAN TRIBES
1:16-18

> [16]And they answered Joshua, "All that you have commanded us we will do, and wherever you send us we will go. [17]Just as we obeyed Moses in all things, so we will obey you; only may the Lord your God be with you, as he was with Moses! [18]Whoever rebels against your commandment and disobeys your words, whatever you command him, shall be put to death. Only be strong and of good courage."

The reply of the Transjordan tribes is not only an acceptance of Joshua's immediate order but especially an acknowledgement of his authority as Moses' successor. The basis of Joshua's authority was the people's belief that the Lord was with him as the Lord was with Moses.

Rahab and the Spies
2:1-24

SPIES ARE SENT TO JERICHO
2:1

> **2** And Joshua the son of Nun sent two men secretly from Shittim as spies, saying, "Go, view the land, especially Jericho." And they went, and came into the house of a harlot whose name was Rahab, and lodged there.

This is one of a number of "spy stories" associated with the conquest (*cf.,* Num 13-14; 21:32; Deut 1:22-25; Josh 7:2-3; Judg 18:2-10). In these stories, the returning spies usually report that the land can be taken by Israelite forces. Their reports then lead to an armed attack followed by Israel's victory. In the Book of Joshua, the account of a military attack against Jericho is suppressed in favor of a story about the miraculous collapse of the city's walls (Josh 6), which resulted in Israel's victory. Despite this suppression, the book does preserve the memory of a conventional battle that was fought between Israel and Jericho (Josh 24:11).

There were then two traditions about Israel's victory over Jericho. One described Jericho's fall in terms of treachery from within and military pressure from without (Josh 2; 6:22-25; 24:11); the other celebrated a miraculous victory wrought by the power of God (Josh 6:1-21). At first these traditions circulated independently of one another. If Jericho were to fall by a miracle, there would be no point to the spies' mission. In fact, such precautions would detract from the dramatic force of the miracle. The attempt to relate the spies' mission with the miraculous defeat of Jericho in Josh 6:17b, 22-25 ignores the fact that since Rahab's house was built into the city wall (Josh 1:15), it would have been destroyed when Jericho's walls collapsed. Despite the differences between them both Josh 2 and 6 attest to the memory that Jericho was captured by Israel.

RAHAB SAVES THE SPIES
2:2-21

²And it was told the king of Jericho, "Behold, certain men of Israel have come here tonight to search out the land." ³Then the king of Jericho sent to Rahab, saying, "Bring forth the men that have come to you, who entered your house; for they have come to search out all the land." ⁴But the woman had taken the two men and hidden them; and she said, "True, men came to me, but I did not know where they came from; ⁵and when the gate was to be closed, at dark, the men went out; where the men went I do not know; pursue them quickly, for you will overtake them." ⁶But she had brought them up to the roof, and hid them with the stalks of flax which she had laid in order on the roof. ⁷So the men pursued after them on the way to the Jordan as far as the fords; and as soon as the pursuers had gone out, the gate was shut.

⁸Before they lay down, she came up to them on the roof, ⁹and said to the men, "I know that the Lord has given you the land, and that the fear of you has fallen upon us, and that all the inhabitants of the land melt away before you. ¹⁰For we have heard how the Lord dried up the water of the Red Sea before you when you came out of Egypt, and what you did to the two kings of the Amorites that were beyond the Jordan, to Sihon and Og, whom you utterly destroyed. ¹¹And as soon as we heard it, our hearts melted, and there was no courage left in any man, because of you; for the Lord your God is he who is God in heaven above and on earth beneath. ¹²Now then, swear to me by the Lord that as I have dealt kindly with you, you also will deal kindly with my father's house, and give me a sure sign, ¹³and save alive my father and mother, my brothers and sisters, and all who belong to them, and deliver our lives from death." ¹⁴And the men said to her, "Our life for yours! If you do not tell this business of ours, then we will deal kindly and faithfully with you when the Lord gives us the land."

¹⁵Then she let them down by a rope through the win-

dow, for her house was built into the city wall, so that she dwelt in the wall. [16]And she said to them, "Go into the hills, lest the pursuers meet you; and hide yourselves there three days, until the pursuers have returned; then afterward you may go your way." [17]The men said to her, "We will be guiltless with respect to this oath of yours which you have made us swear. [18]Behold, when we come into the land, you shall bind this scarlet cord in the window through which you let us down; and you shall gather into your house your father and mother, your brothers, and all your father's household. [19]If any one goes out of the doors of your house into the street, his blood shall be upon his head, and we shall be guiltless; but if a hand is laid upon any one who is with you in the house, his blood shall be on our head. [20]But if you tell this business of ours, then we shall be guiltless with respect to your oath which you have made us swear." [21]And she said, "According to your words, so be it." Then she sent them away, and they departed; and she bound the scarlet cord in the window.

After the spies arrive in Jericho, they go to the house of Rahab to spend the night. Rahab's quick thinking prevents their incursion into Jericho from turning into a disaster. While they are asleep and unaware of the perils that threaten them, the spies are saved by the lies of a prostitute. The text wishes to underscore how dependent Israel was upon the protection of God who often uses the most inappropriate persons to effect the divine will (*cf.,* 1 Sam 16:11; Jer 1:6).

The hand of the Deuteronomistic author is evident in the words of Rahab as she makes an agreement with the spies. Rahab's speech in vv. 9-11 is another montage of Deuteronomic texts (Deut 11:25; 2:3-3:2; 4:39). The author's point should be clear. If the prostitute Rahab shared in the blessings of Israel because of her faith, Israel herself can expect continued blessings if she has the same kind of faith in the God who saves.

Before Rahab lets the spies out of her sight, she extracts a promise of protection from them. The scarlet cord (v. 18) was probably a sign to the invaders of where they will find willing collaborators during their attack. In return for her help, Rahab and her entire family were to be spared during the battle of Jericho. Later it is noted that this promise was kept (Josh 6:25).

THE SPIES REPORT TO JOSHUA
2:22-24

> [22]They departed, and went into the hills, and remained there three days, until the pursuers returned; for the pursuers had made search all along the way and found nothing. [23]Then the two men came down again from the hills, and passed over and came to Joshua the son of Nun; and they told him all that had befallen them. [24]And they said to Joshua, "Truly the Lord has given all the land into our hands; and moreover all the inhabitants of the land are fainthearted because of us."

The story of the spies ends with their escape from Jericho and their report to Joshua. The report underscores a particular emphasis in the biblical story of the conquest as told by the Deuteronomistic author. The taking of the land was the achievement of Israel's God. The conquest could not even begin until the will of God was determined (v. 24). In fact, despite the veneer of activity which is presented in the book (the sending of spies, the arrangement of troops, and actual battles), the impression which the Deuteronomistic author wishes to leave is that Israel was actually passive in the conquest. It was the Lord's doing. For the exiles this was a welcome message since their passivity was not a virtue but a harsh political necessity. If the exiles were ever to return to the land of Israel, it will once again be the Lord's doing.

Israel Crosses the Jordan — A New Era Begins
3:1-5:12

Certainly the crossing of the Jordan River and the entrance into the land of promise were among the most celebrated memories of ancient Israel. These events were recalled in epic narratives and in the rituals of worship. In Josh 3:1-5:12, the Deuteronomistic author combines some of these narrative and liturgical traditions with some of his own reflections in order to help Judah in exile find hope for the future by recalling the stories of her past. Chapters 3 and 4 describe the beginning of a new era in Israel's life and chapter 5 recalls the first Passover celebrated in the new land. The Deuteronomistic author attempted to incite the exiles' faith in God's power to initiate still another new era when all could return to the land of promise and there celebrate the Passover once again.

In this section one can discern three distinct types of material. Certainly the oldest reflects the memories of the military expeditions undertaken by Israel to acquire the land (3:1, 14a, 16; 4:10b, 13, 19b). A second layer shifts the focus from Israel to Yahweh and celebrates the acquisition of the land as a divinely ordained miracle (3:5, 11, 13, 14b-15, 17; 4:2-5, 8-10a, 11-12, 18b-19a, 20-21a, 23). These liturgical formularies portray the entrance into Canaan less as a military adventure and more as a ritual activity since the liturgy celebrated the conquest not as a human achievement but as a manifestation of divine power. The final layer of material contains the reflections of the Deuteronomistic author on the meaning of these events for the people who now found themselves in exile from the land of promise (3:2-4, 6-10; 4:1, 6-7, 14-18a, 21b-22, 24; 5:1).

PREPARATIONS FOR THE CROSSING
3:1-13

3 Early in the morning Joshua rose and set out for Shittim, with all the people of Israel; and they came to the

Jordan, and lodged there before they passed over. ²At the end of three days the officers went through the camp ³and commanded the people, "When you see the ark of the covenant of the Lord your God being carried by the Levitical priests, then you shall set out from your place and follow it, ⁴that you may know the way you shall go, for you have not passed this way before. Yet there shall be a space between you and it, a distance of about two thousand cubits; do not come near it." ⁵And Joshua said to the people, "Sanctify yourselves; for tomorrow the Lord will do wonders among you." ⁶And Joshua said to the priests, "Take up the ark of the covenant, and pass on before the people." And they took up the ark of the covenant, and went before the people.

⁷And the Lord said to Joshua, "This day I will begin to exalt you in the sight of all Israel, that they may know that, as I was with Moses, so I will be with you. ⁸And you shall command the priests who bear the ark of the covenant, 'When you come to the brink of the waters of the Jordan, you shall stand still in the Jordan.'" ⁹And Joshua said to the people of Israel, "Come hither, and hear the words of the Lord your God." ¹⁰And Joshua said, "Hereby you shall know that the living God is among you, and that he will without fail drive out from before you the Canaanites, the Hittites, the Hivites, the Perizzites, the Girgashites, the Amorites, and the Jebusites. ¹¹Behold, the ark of the covenant of the Lord of all the earth is to pass over before you into the Jordan. ¹²Now therefore take twelve men from the tribes of Israel, from each tribe a man. ¹³And when the soles of the feet of the priests who bear the ark of the Lord, the Lord of all the earth, shall rest in the waters of the Jordan, the waters of the Jordan shall be stopped from flowing, and the waters coming down from above shall stand in one heap."

Most of this section (vv. 2-4, 6-10) is the result of the Deuteronomistic edition of the traditions surrounding the crossing of the Jordan. The hand of the Deuteronomistic author is obvious in vv. 2-4 in which the officers relay Joshua's command which was given in the Deuteronomistic introduction to the book (1:10-11). In vv. 3, 6 and 8 the ark is called the "ark of the covenant," Deuteronomy's name for the ark (*cf.*, Deut 10:8; 31:9, 25-26) which it considers to be simply the receptacle for the documents of the covenant (Deut 10:1-5). Another tradition saw the ark as the symbol of God's presence (v. 13; *cf.*, Num 10:33-36; 14:42-44).

The Deuteronomistic author has three concerns in this section. First is the requirement of obedience to the divine directives which prepare Israel not only for the crossing of the Jordan but for the first Passover to be celebrated in her new land. A second concern is the dispossession of the indigenous inhabitants of the land (vv. 9-10). In an apologetic way Deuteronomy justifies this dispossession by reference to the "wickedness" of these nations (Deut 7:17; 9:1, 4-5; 12:2, 29). A third concern is to demonstrate the continuity of divine leadership by making Joshua equal to Moses (v. 7; see also Josh 1:5, 17; 4:14; Deut 1:37f). This identification becomes complete when Joshua is called the "servant of the Lord" (Josh 24:29) which is Deuteronomy's designation of Moses (Deut 31:5).

Since the Deuteronomistic author considered the crossing of the Jordan crucial from a theological point of view, he was determined to make use of the traditions associated with it. He saw the requirement of obedience as the key to Israel's future in her land (Deut 30:15-20). At the time when the Deuteronomistic author wrote, this future appeared to be in doubt yet he is convinced of the continuity of divine leadership and God's continued presence with Israel. In the days of Joshua, the power of God's presence was manifest in the defeat of the nations aligned against Israel (v. 10). This victory of Israel over the nations was inexplicable from a political and military perspective. By retelling this story, the Deuteronomistic author wanted to demonstrate that faith in God's promises is not as foolish as it may appear to be, given the political realities of the 6th century B.C. What God did once for Israel can be done again.

Verses 5, 11 and 13-15 are the remnants of the liturgical commemoration of the crossing. The ritual preparations for the celebrations are prescribed in v. 5 (*cf.,* Exod 10:10-14; Num 11:18). Verses 11, 13-15 form the natural sequence to these preparations.

Verse 12 is out of place in its present context. The purpose of this command will become clear in 4:2-3.

THE MIRACLE
3:14-16a

> [14]So, when the people set out from their tents, to pass over the Jordan with the priests bearing the ark of the covenant before the people, [15]and when those who bore the ark had come to the Jordan, and the feet of the priests bearing the ark were dipped in the brink of the water (the Jordan overflows all its banks throughout the time of harvest), [16]the waters coming down from above stood and rose up in a heap far off, at Adam, the city that is beside Zarethan, and those flowing down toward the sea of the Arabah, the Salt Sea, were wholly cut off;

While the Book of Joshua as a whole attempts to describe the taking of the land as a military expedition of a united Israel under the leadership of Joshua, this pattern is broken here. All martial features are suppressed in favor of a cultic account which portrays the crossing of the Jordan as a liturgical procession led by priests who carry the ark, which never appears elsewhere in the stories of the conquest. The emphasis here is on the miraculous. There is even a parenthetical remark in v. 15b to insure that this emphasis is not lost on the reader since at times the Jordan is fordable without any divine help (Judg 3:28; 8:4; 1 Sam 13:7; 2 Sam 17:24). The account here is reminiscent of the Red Sea crossing (Exod 14-15). This text reflects a liturgical celebration which remembers a miraculous intervention by God with which the taking of the land began.

THE CROSSING
3:16b-5:1

and the people passed over opposite Jericho. [17]And while all Israel were passing over on dry ground, the priests who bore the ark of the covenant of the Lord stood on dry ground in the midst of the Jordan, until all the nation finished passing over the Jordan.

4 When all the nation had finished passing over the Jordan, the Lord said to Joshua, [2]"Take twelve men from the people, from each tribe a man, [3]and command them, 'Take twelve stones from here out of the midst of the Jordan, from the very place where the priests' feet stood, and carry them over with you, and lay them down in the place where you lodge tonight.'" [4]Then Joshua called the twelve men from the people of Israel, whom he had appointed, a man from each tribe; [5]and Joshua said to them, "Pass on before the ark of the Lord your God into the midst of the Jordan, and take up each of you a stone upon his shoulder, according to the number of the tribes of the people of Israel, [6]that this may be a sign among you, when your children ask in time to come, 'What do those stones mean to you?' [7]Then you shall tell them that the waters of the Jordan were cut off before the ark of the covenant of the Lord; when it passed over the Jordan, the waters of the Jordan were cut off. So these stones shall be to the people of Israel a memorial for ever."

[8]And the men of Israel did as Joshua commanded, and took up twelve stones out of the midst of the Jordan, according to the number of the tribes of the people of Israel, as the Lord told Joshua; and they carried them over with them to the place where they lodged, and laid them down there. [9]And Joshua set up twelve stones in the midst of the Jordan, in the place where the feet of the priests bearing the ark of the covenant had stood; and they are there to this day. [10]For the priests who bore the ark stood in the midst of the Jordan, until everything was finished that the Lord commanded Joshua to tell the

people, according to all that Moses had commanded Joshua.

The people passed over in haste; [11]And when all the people had finished passing over, the ark of the Lord and the priests passed over before the people. [12]The sons of Reuben and the sons of Gad and the half-tribe of Manasseh passed over armed before the people of Israel, as Moses had bidden them; [13]about forty thousand ready armed for war passed over before the Lord for battle, to the plains of Jericho. [14]On that day the Lord exalted Joshua in the sight of all Israel; and they stood in awe of him, as they had stood in awe of Moses, all the days of his life.

[15]And the Lord said to Joshua, [16]"Command the priests who bear the ark of the testimony to come up out of the Jordan." [17]Joshua therefore commanded the priests, "Come up out of the Jordan." [18]And when the priests bearing the ark of the covenant of the Lord came up from the midst of the Jordan, and the soles of the priests' feet were lifed up on dry ground, the waters of the Jordan returned to their place and overflowed all its banks, as before.

[19]The people came up out of the Jordan on the tenth day of the first month, and they encamped at Gilgal on the east border of Jericho. [20]And those twelve stones, which they took out of the Jordan, Joshua set up in Gilgal. [21]And he said to the people of Israel, "When your children ask their fathers in time to come, 'What do these stones mean?' [22]then you shall let your children know, 'Israel passed over this Jordan on dry ground.' [23]For the Lord your God dried up the waters of the Jordan for you until you passed over, as the Lord your God did to the Red Sea, which he dried up for us until we passed over, [24]so that all the peoples of the earth may know that the hand of the Lord is mighty; that you may fear the Lord your God for ever."

5 When all the kings of the Amorites that were beyond the Jordan to the west, and all the kings of the Canaanites

that were by the sea, heard that the Lord had dried up the waters of the Jordan for the people of Israel until they had crossed over, their heart melted, and there was no longer any spirit in them, because of the people of Israel.

Only a single allusion to the military aspect of the entrance into Canaan has survived in this unit (4:13). The earlier account of the crossing has been successfully "demilitarized" and replaced with descriptions of a liturgical action and the erection of memorial stones. The Deuteronomistic author felt quite at ease with this approach since he preferred a presentation which emphasized the mighty acts of God and underplayed the bravery and cunning of Israel's warriors. After all, the land was not as prize won by Israel's armies; it was a *gift* of God to Israel (Deut 1:5 and *passim*).

The unit preserves three cultic traditions connected with the crossing of the Jordan: one about memorial stones set up at Gilgal (4:1-3, 6-7, 8b, 20), a second about memorial stones placed in the Jordan itself (4:4-5, 8a, 9, 15-19) and a third tradition about the ark (3:17; 4:7, 9, 16, 18). These three traditions have been combined rather clumsily. The result is a number of inconsistencies and repetitions. Unfortunately no one tradition remained intact so that it is impossible to know what really happened. One conclusion that may be drawn from these liturgical traditions is that Gilgal (vv. 19-20) may have been the sanctuary at which the tribes celebrated their entrance into Canaan just as Shechem appears to have been the sanctuary at which the tribes commemorated the Sinai event (Deut 27; Josh 24).

Despite the lack of clarity in the unit as it now stands, the emphases of the Deuteronomistic author are clear. First is the concern that future generations learn of God's fidelity by hearing this story (4:6-7, 21-24). Secondly the inclusion of the Transjordan tribes in the crossing (vv. 12-13) preserves the Deuteronomistic presentation of the conquest as an all-Israelite affair. As in Josh 3:7, the continuity of divine guidance over Israel is assured in the person of Joshua (4:14). Finally the effect of the miraculous crossing is to inspire awe among the nations (4:24-5:1). The Lord is to be seen as God not only by Israel but by all nations.

THE FIRST PASSOVER IN THE LAND
5:2-12

The Preparations
5:2-9

> [2]At that time the Lord said to Joshua, "Make flint knives and circumcise the people of Israel again the second time." [3]So Joshua made flint knives, and circumcised the people of Israel at Gibeath-haaraloth. [4]And this is the reason why Joshua circumcised them: all the males of the people who came out of Egypt, all the men of war, had died on the way in the wilderness after they had come out of Egypt. [5]Though all the people who came out had been circumcised, yet all the people that were born on the way in the wilderness after they had come out of Egypt had not been circumcised. [6]For the people of Israel walked forty years in the wilderness, till all the nations, the men of war that came forth out of Egypt, perished, because they did not hearken to the voice of the Lord; to them the Lord swore that he would not let them see the land which the Lord had sworn to their fathers to give us, a land flowing with milk and honey. [7]So it was their children, whom he raised up in their stead, that Joshua circumcised; for they were uncircumcised, because they had not been circumcised on the way.
>
> [8]When the circumcising of all the nations was done, they remained in their places in the camp till they were healed. [9]And the Lord said to Joshua, "This day I have rolled away the reproach of Egypt from you." And so the name of that place is called Gilgal to this day.

Exod 12:48 makes it clear that circumcision was required of all males who were to participate in the Passover celebration. Verses 2-3 and 8-9 describe this ritual as being performed just after Israel arrives in the land. The site of this ceremony was the "Hill of Foreskins" (v. 3), probably a well known site near Gilgal and the logical setting for this story.

The ritual of circumcision was, at one time, a practice common to a number of nations in the ancient Near East. In Israel it took on increasing importance until it was seen as a sign of Israel's unique relationship to God (Gen 17:11-13). Certainly by the time of the Exile, circumcision became a confession of faith in the Lord.

The Deuteronomistic author uses this story to preach to the Exiles. Perhaps he formulated the curious command in v. 2. Here the Lord tells Joshua to circumcise Israel "again the second time." Those words signified a fresh start for Israel in the land once the Exile ended. Certainly the Deuteronomist is responsible for vv. 4-7, an apologetic digression which becomes a homily on disobedience and its consequences.

The etiology of Gilgal (v. 9) and its supposed connection with the "rolling back" of the reproach of Egypt are obscure. Perhaps this reproach refers to the abject social status of Israel in Egypt. With the entrance into the new land the stigma of slavery has been removed forever and replaced by the mark of Israel's covenant with God.

The Passover
5:10-12

10While the people of Israel were encamped in Gilgal they kept the passover on the fourteenth day of the month at evening in the plains of Jericho. 11And on the morrow after the passover, on that very day, they ate of the produce of the land, unleavened cakes and parched grain. 12And the manna ceased on the morrow, when they ate of the produce of the land; and the people of Israel had manna no more, but ate of the fruit of the land of Canaan that year.

The ceremony connected with the observance of Israel's first Passover in the new land is not described; however, the significance of the celebration is obvious. Israel now begins her new life in the land of promise. The manna is no longer necessary since Israel can live off the produce of her land. The time of wandering in the wilderness has just ended; the time of conquest is about to begin.

The Story Of The Conquest In Central Canaan
5:13-8:35

A THEOPHANY
5:13-15

> [13]When Joshua was by Jericho, he lifted up his eyes and looked, and behold, a man stood before him with his drawn sword in his hand; and Joshua went to him and said to him, "Are you for us, or for our adversaries?" [14]And he said, "No; but as commander of the army of the Lord I have now come." And Joshua fell on his face to the earth, and worshipped, and said to him, "What does my lord bid his servant?" [15]And the commander of the Lord's army said to Joshua, "Put off your shoes from your feet; for the place where you stand is holy." And Joshua did so.

The story of the conquest begins with a theophany. This section originally belonged to a tradition which remembered the victory over Jericho as the result of a military campaign (*cf.,* Josh 2; 6:22-25; 24:11). The text provided not only the divine warrant for that campaign but also the assurance of divine leadership as it is being conducted. In a subsequent tradition about the victory over Jericho, the military victory and the treachery of Rahab which expedited it were absorbed into a story of a miraculous victory (Josh 6:1-21).

From the Deuteronomistic perspective a most important emphasis in this text is the divine sanction for Joshua's leadership. Apparently these verses are to be understood as Joshua's "call." They are reminiscent of the theophany that accompanied the call of Moses (Exod 3:1-22). In fact v. 15 is a direct quote of Exod 3:5. Joshua is indeed the divinely appointed successor of Moses.

THE FALL OF JERICHO
6:1-27

Despite the complex character of this chapter, the final editor has succeeded in presenting a well ordered story about the taking of Jericho. A close reading of Josh 6 reveals some irregularities. Do the walls fall because of the trumpet blasts or the people's shouts? Do the priests blow the trumpets or does the rear guard do so? Are the trumpets to be blown each day or only on the seventh day? The translators of the Septuagint version attempted to smooth out the confusion by eliminating some of the repetitious elements. As a result, the Greek text of Josh 6 is somewhat shorter than the Hebrew text reproduced here in translation. Since this chapter of Joshua does have a complicated literary history, reconstructing that history is not simple. What can be discerned with relative ease is the shape of the story as the final editor has presented it along with the theological assumptions behind the presentation.

The story of Jericho's fall has been shaped by the Holy War ideology of the Deuteronomic tradition (*cf.,* Deut 20). While there may have been a secular tradition surrounding the taking of Jericho (the march of the people's army and their shouts augmented by elements of a liturgical tradition which celebrated the fall of the city (the Ark, the priests, the procession with trumpets), Josh 6 wishes to portray the fall of Jericho as an act of Holy War. This is clear from the very structure of this chapter.

The Introduction
6:1

⁶Now Jericho was shut up from within and from without because of the people of Israel; none went out, and none came in.

Archaeological investigation in the region of Jericho has led to the conclusion that the site was a rather insignificant settlement during the Late Bronze Age (1500-1200 B.C.), the period of the Israelite "conquest." There is no indication that any walls date from the Late Bronze Age. The inhabitants of Jericho during that period, however, may have used what remained of the walls of Middle Bronze Age Jericho which was destroyed and abandoned in 1550 B.C. Even though Jericho may have had little or no fortifications in the period of the Israelite settlement, the town had to be neutralized before the Israelite tribes could make secure incursions into the highlands to the west. What follows in Josh 6 is an epic-like description of the first battle fought by the Israelite tribes in Canaan.

The Lord's Instruction
6:2-5

> ²And the Lord said to Joshua, "See, I have given into your hand Jericho, with its king and mighty men of valor. ³You shall march around the city once. Thus shall you do for six days. ⁴And seven priests shall bear seven trumpets of rams' horns before the ark; and on the seventh day you shall march around the city seven times, the priests blowing the trumpets. ⁵And when they make a long blast with the ram's horn, as soon as you hear the sound of the trumpet, then all the people shall shout with a great shout; and the wall of the city will fall down flat, and the people shall go up every man straight before him."

Deut 20:1-4 makes it clear that Holy War is not a human enterprise. While the nations have horses and chariots, Israel has the Lord who gives victory. The instructions given by God to Joshua show how the Lord will achieve victory in the conflict with Jericho. These instructions describe a liturgical action rather than a military stratagem. "...I have given into your hand Jericho..." (v. 2a) is a formulaic expression signifying that victory in Holy War is accomplished by the Divine Will (*cf.*, Deut 20:13a). The expression is common in stories reflecting the Holy War ideology. The text certainly means to describe a miracle: the walls of Jericho collapse due to the performance of a ritual action ordered by God. The fall of Jericho and the means of its accomplishment are really paradigms of the "conquest." Israel's acquisition of the land which was to be the scene of her subsequent history did not occur by means of any human achievement. It was a divine gift.

Joshua's Instructions
6:6-7

> [6]So Joshua the son of Nun called the priests and said to them, "Take up the ark of the covenant, and let seven priests bear seven trumpets of rams' horns before the ark of the Lord." [7]And he said to the people, "Go forward; march around the city, and let the armed men pass on before the ark of the Lord."

In his position as Moses' successor, Joshua relays the commands of God to the priests and people who are to carry them out. While the Lord alone gives victory, Israel's obedience to the Divine Will is necessary for her to be successful in her efforts to take possession of the land. As vv. 8-21 will show, there is no human force that can stop Israel when she is obedient to the commands of the Lord. On the other hand, the next unit (Josh 7-8) demonstrates the reverse: Israel cannot be victorious when there is any disobedience.

God's Instructions Are Executed
6:8-21

> [8]And as Joshua had commanded the people, the seven priests bearing the seven trumpets of rams' horns before the Lord went forward, blowing the trumpets, with the ark of the covenant of the Lord following them. [9]And the armed men went before the priests who blew the trumpets, and the rear guard came after the ark, while the trumpets blew continually. [10]But Joshua commanded the

people, "You shall not shout or let your voice be heard, neither shall any word go out of your mouth, until the day I bid you shout; then you shall shout." [11]So he caused the ark of the Lord to compass the city, going about it once; and they came into the camp, and spent the night in the camp.

[12]Then Joshua rose early in the morning, and the priests took up the ark of the Lord. [13]And the seven priests bearing the seven trumpets of rams' horns before the ark of the Lord passed on, blowing the trumpets continually; and the armed men went before them, and the rear guard came after the ark of the Lord, while the trumpets blew continually. [14]And the second day they marched around the city once, and returned into the camp. So they did for six days.

[15]On the seventh day they rose early at the dawn of day, and marched around the city in the same manner seven times: it was only on that day that they marched around the city seven times. [16]And at the seventh time, when the priests had blown the trumpets, Joshua said to the people, "Shout; for the Lord has given you the city. [17]And the city and all that is within it shall be devoted to the Lord for destruction; only Rahab the harlot and all who are with her in her house shall live, because she hid the messengers that we sent. [18]But you, keep yourselves from the things devoted to destruction, lest when you have devoted them you take any of the devoted things and make the camp of Israel a thing for destruction, and bring trouble upon it. [19]But all silver and gold, and vessels of bronze and iron, are sacred to the Lord; they shall go into the treasury of the Lord." [20]So the people shouted, and the trumpets were blown. As soon as the people heard the sound of the trumpet, the people raised a great shout, and the wall fell down flat, so that the people went up into the city, every man straight before him, and they took the city. [21]Then they utterly destroyed all in the city, both men and women, young and old, oxen, sheep, and asses, with the edge of the sword.

The basic assumption of Deuteronomic theology is that obedience always redounds to Israel's benefit. Here without any questions or doubts, Israel proceeds to attack Jericho with a liturgical procession! Because the tribes did exactly as God commanded them through Joshua, their victory over Jericho was complete. For the Deuteronomists this is a basic law of life: obedience brings blessing.

According to Deut 20:16-17, the inhabitants of a captured city plus their possessions belonged to the Lord. According to v. 21, the Israelites recognized these as the property of God by killing Jericho's inhabitants and their livestock. Because they were the property of God, they were unsafe for human use. They had to be destroyed. Perhaps this practice was part of Israel's Semitic cultural inheritance. Extra-biblical evidence describes the same type of utter destruction as being carried out against Israel by Moab.

That the rules of Holy War could be modified is apparent from v. 17b. While Moses sees no exception from the complete destruction of a captured city and its inhabitants (Deut 20:16), Joshua makes an exception for Rahab and her family. Joshua's mercy towards Rahab is considered to be a legitimate exception to the Law. Just as God was merciful in giving Israel her land (Deut 9-10) so Joshua is merciful in giving Rahab and her family a share in that inheritance.

The Aftermath of Victory
6:22-27

²²And Joshua said to the two men who had spied out the land, "Go into the harlot's house, and bring out from it the woman, and all who belong to her, as you swore to her." ²³So the young men who had been spies went in, and brought out Rahab, and her father and mother and brothers and all who belonged to her; and they brought all her kindred, and set them outside the camp of Israel. ²⁴And they burned the city with fire, and all within it; only the silver and gold, and the vessels of bronze and of iron, they put into the treasury of the house of the Lord. ²⁵But Rahab the harlot, and her father's household, and all who

belonged to her, Joshua saved alive; and she dwelt in Israel to this day, because she hid the messengers whom Joshua sent to spy out Jericho.

²⁶Joshua laid an oath upon them at that time, saying, "Cursed before the Lord be the man that rises up and rebuilds this city, Jericho.

At the cost of his first-born shall he
    lay its foundation,
and at the cost of his youngest son
    shall he set up its gates."

²⁷So the Lord was with Joshua; and his fame was in all the land.

This section contains another account of Rahab's rescue during the fall of Jericho (vv. 22-23) and a second description of the destruction of the city (v. 24). The reference to the "house of the Lord"(v. 24b) may be an anachronism if this is a reference to the Temple. Of course, the Temple was not to be built until the time of Solomon more than 200 years later.

The text ends with two etiologies. The first (v. 25) explains why some Canaanites survived the destruction of Jericho; the second (v. 26) explains why the town of Jericho remained in ruins until the 7th century (*cf.*, 1 Kg 16:34 which describes one attempt to rebuild Jericho). Other texts, Josh 18:21 and 2 Sam 10:5, do show that the region near Jericho did remain inhabited to some extent after the entrance of the Israelite tribes into Canaan.

The description of the fall of Jericho does reflect historical memories surrounding Israel's entrance into Canaan, though the basis of these memories cannot be determined with precision. This first battle in the new land is related in epic proportions and is given a sacral character. This account celebrates God's gift of the land to Israel, an important theme in the Deuteronomistic History. When Israel found herself removed from that land in exile, this text became a powerful illustration of how obedience was the way Israel acquired her land and the only way Israel could re-acquire it.

THE FALL OF AI
7:1-8:35

This unit presents the taking of Ai in two stages. The first ends in failure (7:2-5); the second with success (8:1-29). The failure is explained by the intervening story concerning Achan's sin following the conquest of Jericho (7:1, 6-26). What appears to be a single unified narrative is really the result of combining two different stories: one concerning Achan and a second concerning Ai. The latter can be read quite independently of the former. In fact 8:2, 27 allows Israel to keep a portion of the booty from Ai — the very crime for which Israel is punished in 7:1. Secondly the scene of Achan's execution (7:25-27) is a long way from both Ai and Jericho, which leads to the conclusion that the connection between Ai, Jericho and Achan is artificial.

The original form of the story concerning the taking of Ai dealt with a defeat of the Israelite forces which was later reversed by means of a clever ruse. Originally the Achan story was probably the result of explaining the name of the Achor Valley (7:24) and the large pile of stone that was a familiar sight there (7:26). Both traditions probably circulated among the tribe of Benjamin at first. Achan was a member of the tribe of Judah and preserving his story served to fuel the rivalry between these two tribes. The Ai tradition originally intended to point to Benjamin's role in the conquest since Ai is located in the hill country of Benjamin.

These two independent traditions were rather cleverly combined under the force of the Israelite belief which held that the conquest was the work of God despite any human endeavor. Independent tribal traditions surrounding the conquest were combined and presented in such a way as to acknowledge and emphasize Yahweh's role in the acquisition of Israel's land.

For the Deuteronomistic editor this combined narrative supported his views that the obedience of faith provided Israel with victory. Disobedience always brings disaster — whether that disaster be defeat at Ai or the Exile. To bring this narrative into complete harmony with his views the

Deuteronomist made the battle at Ai into a "Holy War." In such a war obedience and not strategy is decisive.

Achan's Sin
7:1

> 7   But the people of Israel broke faith in regard to the devoted things; for Achan the son of Carmi, son of Zabdi, son of Zerah, of the tribe of Judah, took some of the devoted things; and the anger of the Lord burned against the people of Israel.

The opening verse of these two chapters is an editorial devise whose purpose is to connect the stories of Achan and Ai with the just concluded account of Jericho's fall. It anticipates the stories to follow by indicating that Achan's sin has turned the Lord against Israel. The reader then is led to consider the defeat at Ai as the result of Achan's sin even before the narrative itself makes that conclusion clear.

Initial Defeat
7:2-5

> ²Joshua sent men from Jericho to Ai, which is near Bethaven, east of Bethel, and said to them, "Go up and spy out the land." And the men went up and spied out Ai. ³And they returned to Joshua, and said to him, "Let not all the people go up, but let about two or three thousand men go up and attack Ai; do not make the whole people toil up there, for they are but few." ⁴So about three thousand went up there from the people; and they fled before the men of Ai, ⁵and the men of Ai killed about thirty-six men of them, and chased them before the gate as far as Shebarim, and slew them at the descent. And the hearts of the people melted, and became as water.

An overly optimistic report from the spies sent to study Ai's defenses is cited as the cause of Israel's defeat. On the basis of that report too small of a force was sent against the defenders of the city. The Israelite invaders encounter these defenders at the city gate and suffer a disheartening defeat. Certainly such an experience was common enough during the initial stages of Israel's move against the powerful Canaanite city-states. This defeat is remembered to set the stage for the stratagem devised to lead the Israelite tribes to eventual victory. There is no hint here of any other cause for failure except that of faulty military intelligence.

Israel's Lament
7:6-9

> 6Then Joshua rent his clothes, and fell to the earth upon his face before the ark of the Lord until the evening, he and the elders of Israel; and they put dust upon their heads. 7And Joshua said, "Alas, O Lord God, why hast thou brought this people over the Jordan at all, to give us into the hands of the Amorites, to destroy us? Would that we had been content to dwell beyond the Jordan! 8O Lord, what can I say, when Israel has turned their backs before their enemies! 9For the Canaanites and all the inhabitants of the land will hear of it, and will surround us, and cut off our name from the earth, and what wilt thou do for thy great name?"

Following the rout of the Israelite forces, the leaders of the tribes participate in a ritual of mourning and lamentation. Here the blame for Israel's loss at Ai is laid squarely at the feet of Yahweh who should be leading Israel to victory rather than defeat. Joshua suggests that any more Israelite defeats will compromise the very honor of God. If Israel is destroyed, what will God do for worshippers! The same motif is found in the psalms of lament. It demonstrates Israel's approach to the experience of God's absence. This approach is not one of resignation but of confrontation. In the face of defeat, Israel demands that Yahweh act like God!

Yahweh's Answer
7:10-15

> [10]The Lord said to Joshua, "Arise, why have you thus fallen upon your face? [11]Israel has sinned; they have transgressed my covenant which I commanded them; they have taken some of the devoted things; they have stolen, and lied, and put them among their own stuff. [12]Therefore the people of Israel cannot stand before their enemies; they turn their backs before their enemies, because they have become a thing for destruction. I will be with you no more, unless you destroy the devoted things from among you. [13]Up, sanctify the people, and say, 'Sanctify yourselves for tomorrow; for thus says the Lord, God of Israel, "There are devoted things in the midst of you, O Israel; you cannot stand before your enemies, until you take away the devoted things from among you." [14]In the morning therefore you shall be brought near by your tribes; and the tribe which the Lord takes shall come near by families; and the family which the Lord takes shall come near by households; and the household which the Lord takes shall come near man by man. [15]And he who is taken with the devoted things shall be burned with fire, he and all that he has, because he has transgressed the covenant of the Lord, and because he has done a shameful thing in Israel.'"

In response to the prayer of lamentation, God reveals the true cause of Israel's defeat: the theft of booty from Jericho. This was not permitted in a Holy War. To remedy this situation the guilty party had to be identified and punished. The assumption is that evil performed even by a single individual has effects far beyond the individual's own person. Certainly this is a very sophisticated understanding of the power of evil. Israel's future will always be in doubt as long as disobedience goes unchecked. The means of identifying the guilty party is through casting of lots, a common procedure in determining the divine will (*cf.,* Josh 14:2; 18:6; 1 Sam 10:19-24; Jon 1:7; Acts 1:26).

Sin Exposed and Expunged
7:16-25

[16]So Joshua rose early in the morning, and brought Israel near tribe by tribe, and the tribe of Judah was taken; [17]and he brought near the families of Judah, and the family of the Zerahites was taken; and he brought near the family of the Zerahites man by man, and Zabdi was taken; [18]and he brought near his household man by man, and Achan the son of Carmi, son of Zabdi, son of Zerah, of the tribe of Judah, was taken. [19]Then Joshua said to Achan, "My son, give glory to the Lord God of Israel, and render praise to him; and tell me now what you have done; do not hide it from me." [20]And Achan answered Joshua, "Of a truth I have sinned against the Lord God of Israel, and this is what I did: [21]when I saw among the spoil a beautiful mantle from Shinar, and two hundred shekels of silver, and a bar of gold weighing fifty shekels, then I coveted them, and took them; and behold, they are hidden in the earth inside my tent, with the silver underneath."

[22]So Joshua sent messengers, and they ran to the tent; and behold, it was hidden in his tent with the silver underneath. [23]And they took them out of the tent and brought them to Joshua and all the people of Israel; and they laid them down before the Lord. [24]And Joshua and all Israel with him took Achan the son of Zerah, and the silver and the mantle and the bar of gold, and his sons and daughters, and his oxen and asses and sheep, and his tent, and all that he had; and they brought them up to the Valley of Achor. [25]And Joshua said, "Why did you bring trouble on us? The Lord brings trouble on you today." And all Israel stoned him with stones; they burned them with fire, and stoned them with stones.

With Israel's very fate hanging in the balance, her tribes, clans and families are subjected to the lot until Achan is revealed to be the one guilty of theft. The tension breaks as Achan confesses his crime and even provides a list of what he has stolen. The stolen booty is recovered and the criminal is executed. There was no other way of dealing with Achan's sin. Once Achan took the booty, he set in motion a process that inevitably led to his own destruction and threatened the very existence of Israel. This insight represents a very sophisticated understanding of the destructive power of evil.

Achan's Sin Remembered
7:26

> [26]And they raised over him a great heap of stones that remains to this day; then the Lord turned from his burning anger. Therefore to this day the name of that place is called the Valley of Achor.

The story of Achan ends with an etiology of the great pile of stones found in the Achor Valley. The names Achan and Achor are a word-play in Hebrew on the word "trouble" (v. 25): "Why did you bring *trouble* on us?" It was this impressive heap of stones in the Achor Valley which kept this story of early Israel's "trouble" alive for later generations.

Yahweh's instructions and Joshua's preparations
8:1-9

> **8** And the Lord said to Joshua, "Do not fear or be dismayed; take all the fighting men with you, and arise, go up to Ai; see, I have given into your hand the king of Ai, and his people, his city, and his land; [2]and you shall do to Ai and its king as you did to Jericho and its king; only its spoil and its cattle you shall take as booty for yourselves; lay an ambush against the city, behind it."
>
> [3]So Joshua arose, and all the fighting men, to go up to Ai; and Joshua chose thirty thousand mighty men of valor, and sent them forth by night. [4]And he commanded them, "Behold, you shall lie in ambush against the city, behind it; do not go very far from the city, but hold yourselves all in readiness; [5]and I, and all the people who are with me, will approach the city. And when they come

out against us, as before, we shall flee before them; [6]and
they will come out after us, till we have drawn them away
from the city; for they will say, 'They are fleeing from us,
as before.' So we will flee from them; [7]then you shall rise
up from the ambush, and seize the city; for the Lord your
God will give it into your hand. [8]And when you have
taken the city, you shall set the city on fire, doing as the
Lord has bidden; see, I have commanded you." [9]So
Joshua sent them forth; and they went to the place of
ambush, and lay between Bethel and Ai, to the west of Ai;
but Joshua spent that night among the people.

The story of Ai's fall is resumed here. Together with 7:2-5,
this account of Israel's conquest of Ai is a detailed and
highly probable report of a military expedition. The elements of Holy War are kept to a minimum (v. 1, 7b, 18, 27).
Except for these few references to God's role in the taking of
Ai, the account is without any miraculous elements. Even
the liturgical features (priests, processions with the Ark,
trumpet blasts) which were so prominent in the Jericho
story are missing here. The victory over Ai is presented as
the result of Joshua's strategy.

The Attack
8:10-27

[10]And Joshua arose early in the morning and mustered
the people, and went up, with the elders of Israel, before
the people of Ai. [11]And all the fighting men who were
with him went up, and drew near before the city, and
encamped on the north side of Ai, with a ravine between
them and Ai. [12]And he took about five thousand men,
and set them in ambush between Bethel and Ai, to the
west of the city. [13]So they stationed the forces, the main
encampment which was north of the city and its rear
guard west of the city. But Joshua spent that night in the
valley. [14]And when the king of Ai saw this he and all his
people, the men of the city, made haste and went out early
to the descent toward the Arabah to meet Israel in battle;

but he did not know that there was an ambush against him behind the city. [15]And Joshua and all Israel made a pretense of being beaten before them, and fled in the direction of the wilderness. [16]So all the people who were in the city were called together to pursue them, and as they pursued Joshua they were drawn away from the city. [17]There was not a man left in Ai or Bethel, who did not go out after Israel; they left the city open, and pursued Israel.

[18]Then the Lord said to Joshua, "Stretch out the javelin that is in your hand toward Ai; for I will give it into your hand." And Joshua stretched out the javelin that was in his hand toward the city. [19]And the ambush rose quickly out of their place, and as soon as he had stretched out his hand, they ran and entered the city and took it; and they made haste to set the city on fire. [20]So when the men of Ai looked back, behold, the smoke of the city went up to heaven; and they had no power to flee this way or that, for the people that fled to the wilderness turned back upon the pursuers. [21]And when Joshua and all Israel saw that the ambush had taken the city, and that the smoke of the city went up, then they turned back and smote the men of Ai. [22]And the others came forth from the city against them; so they were in the midst of Israel, some on this side, and some on that side; and Israel smote them, until there was left none that survived or escaped. [23]But the king of Ai they took alive, and brought him to Joshua.

[24]When Israel had finished slaughtering all the inhabitants of Ai in the open wilderness where they pursued them, and all of them to the very last had fallen by the edge of the sword, all Israel returned to Ai, and smote it with the edge of the sword. [25]And all who fell that day, both men and women, were twelve thousand, all the people of Ai. [26]For Joshua did not draw back his hand, with which he stretched out the javelin, until he had utterly destroyed all the inhabitants of Ai. [27]Only the cattle and the spoil of that city Israel took as their booty, according to the word of the Lord which he commanded Joshua.

The body of the narrative is a description of how Joshua's plan was executed. An elite force of Israelite troops secretly advances to a position west of Ai. Joshua and the main force encamp directly in front of the city. The king of Ai responds to this provocation by leading his own troops against the Israelites. The king expected to make short work of the invaders. Joshua plays on the confidence of Ai's forces by leading the Israelites in a retreat which draws Ai's defenders farther and farther from the city. The elite force of Israelite troops enters Ai and sets it ablaze. This is a signal to Joshua's main force to turn around. The king of Ai and his army found themselves caught in Israelite pincers. The army was massacred; the king was captured and later executed.

The victory remembered
8:28-29

[28]So Joshua burned Ai, and made it for ever a heap of ruins, as it is to this day. [29]And he hanged the king of Ai on a tree until evening; and at the going down of the sun Joshua commanded, and they took his body down from the tree, and cast it at the entrance of the gate of the city, and raised over it a great heap of stones, which stands there to this day.

The narrative ends with two etiologies dealing with the ruins of Ai itself and the heap of stones outside the city which marked the grave of Ai's king. Both these remained as symbols that Israel acquired the land by force of arms. As pilgrims travelled to and from the shrines at Bethel and Gilgal, these ruins stood as stark reminders of Israel's conquest of her land.

While the exact location of ancient Ai is not definitively known, archaeological excavation in the location suggested by the Biblical narrative indicates that no city existed at the time of the Israelite conquest. Excavations have revealed a city which was destroyed approximately 2400 B.C. (over a thousand years before the entrance of the Israelite tribes into Canaan.) The city was not rebuilt until 1200 B.C. The narrative as it now stands is not historically authentic except with regard to the fact that the Israelite settlement in Canaan was achieved, in part, by military conquest. This may explain why the narrative is not aware of the city's name. Throughout the story the city conquered by Israel is called "the ruin." (Ai means ruin in Hebrew.)

In its present form, this story focuses the reader's attention on the famous "ruin" that was located in the territory of Benjamin. The details of Josh 8 are remarkably similar to those of another story about the same tribe in Judg 20. In the latter narrative, the Benjaminites are defeated. In Josh 8 the tribe's storytellers use the famous ruin in their territory to reverse the damage done to their tribe's prestige.

The altar on Mt. Ebal
8:30-35

[30]Then Joshua built an altar on Mount Ebal to the Lord, the God of Israel, [31]as Moses the servant of the Lord had commanded the people of Israel, as it is written in the book of the law of Moses, "an altar of unhewn stones, upon which no man has lifted an iron tool"; and they offered on it burnt offerings to the Lord, and sacrificed peace offerings. [32]And there, in the presence of the people of Israel, he wrote upon the stones a copy of the law of Moses, which he had written. [33]And all Israel, sojourner as well as homeborn, with their elders and officers and their judges, stood on opposite sides of the ark before the Levitical priests who carried the ark of the covenant of the Lord, half of them in front of Mount Gerizim and half of them in front of Mount Ebal, as Moses the servant of the Lord had commanded at the first, that they should bless the people of Israel. [34]And afterward he read all the words of the law, the blessing and the curse, according to all that is written in the book of the law. [35]There was not a word of all that Moses commanded which Joshua did not read before all the assembly of Israel, and the women, and the little ones, and the sojourners who lived among them.

The Gibeonite affair described in the next chapter serves as a natural sequence to the narrative about the fall of Ai to the Israelite forces. The presence of 8:30-35 between these two stories is anomalous. According to these passages the Israelite tribes travel about 20 miles northward from Ai to Shechem in order to erect an altar on Mt. Ebal. They then must retrace their steps southward for another 20 miles in order to encamp at Gilgal (9:6). The Septuagint places this passage after 9:2 yet the difficulty remains. Recent commentators have suggested that this passage originally followed 24:27. Certainly the building of an altar on Mt. Ebal would have formed a fitting conclusion to Joshua's final speech delivered at Shechem and recounted in chapter 24.

How then did this passage come to be detached from chapter 24 and placed within its present context? At first the account of Ai's fall may have concluded with the establishment of an Israelite cult center at Bethel which was in the immediate vicinity of Ai. This would parallel the story about the crossing of the Jordan which concluded with an etiology of the cult center at Gilgal (4-5). In the eyes of the Deuteronomistic author, the cult center of Bethel was discredited by Jeroboam I's attempt to use it in order to deflect the allegiance of the Northern Kingdom from the Davidic dynasty and the Jerusalem Temple (*cf.*, 1 Kgs 12:26-33). The editor substitutes a narrative about the Shechem sanctuary whose legitimacy is guaranteed by Deut 11, 27 and 31.

The narrative serves another purpose for the Deuteronomist since he uses it to present Joshua as a model for all Israel. While it is true that Joshua succeeds Moses as the leader of the tribes, the Deuteronomist does not really portray Joshua as another Moses; he is rather Israel in microcosm. Joshua is to do just what Israel is to do: carry out the commands of God which have been transmitted through Moses and recorded in the "law of Moses" (v. 32). The success that Joshua enjoys is quite understandable and even predictable. The Deuteronomist believed that the Law together with its blessings and curses continued in validity and efficacy down to his own day. In his eyes Israel's troubles are as understandable and predictable as were Joshua's successes. To reverse her situation all Israel had to do was to be as obedient in her circumstances as was Joshua in his. The message of this passage is clear: "Follow the lead of Joshua!"

The Conquest in the South
9:1-10:43

ISRAEL FACES A UNITED ENEMY
9:1-2

> **9** When all the kings who were beyond the Jordan in the hill country and in the lowland all along the coast of the Great Sea toward Lebanon, the Hittites, the Amorites, the Canaanites, the Perizzites, the Hivites, and the Jebusites, heard of this, ²they gathered together with one accord to fight Joshua and Israel.

This brief statement introduces a change of scene in the Book of Joshua from the central region of Canaan to the South (vv. 9-10) and then to the North (vv. 11). While these verses speak of a great coalition of the Canaanite city-states west of the Jordan, the remainder of the Book of Joshua does not portray Israel as ever having to face such a united enemy. This transitional piece, which is probably the result of editorial work, shows how the events of the remote past are remembered — usually with some exaggeration.

THE TREATY WITH GIBEON
9:3-27

Unlike the cases of Jericho and Ai, archaeology has been able to determine that Gibeon was occupied during the period of the Israelite entrance into Canaan. Unfortunately the literary problems of this text make up for the comparative ease with which the archaeological data can be handled.

The trickster motif which is at the core of this story argues for the antiquity of the narrative and is reminiscent of similar folk-tales in Genesis (*cf.*, Gen 27, 30, 34). On the other hand, the Deuteronomic phraseology in vv. 9b-10, 24a, 25 (*cf.,* Deut 20:10-18) and especially the allusion to the Jerusalem Temple in v. 27 (*cf.,* Deut 12:5) shows that the final form of this passage is relatively late. Similarly the inconsistencies and duplications which abound here underscore the complexity of the literary questions which have surrounded this text. For example, v. 9 repeats v. 6 and vv. 12-13 repeat vv. 4-5. In v. 15 Joshua makes peace with the Gibeonites while according to v. 18 the "leaders of the congregation" do so. Similarly in v. 21 the "leaders of the congregation" determine the future status of the Gibeonites while in vv. 23, 27 Joshua does so. Exactly how this passage passed through the many hands responsible for it is not an easy question to answer.

Though the literary problems may be insoluble, the theological thrust of the passage is clear enough. It intends to explain how and why the norms of Holy War were not followed in the case of the Gibeonites. Theoretically Israel was to acquire her land by force of arms and through the extermination of Canaan's indigenous population. Of course, no such extermination ever took place and this text demonstrates that the Israelite settlement went forward at times without armed conflict. In the course of describing the conquest, the Book of Joshua presents the requirements of Holy War as being mutable: Rahab is spared, booty from Ai is kept, and now the Gibeonites are incorporated into Israel. While the will of the Lord as formulated in the Book of the Law is to be the guide for Israel's life, even this Law has to be interpreted humanely — not mechanistically. Obedience to the Law is indeed the way to life, but that obedience has a certain dialogical character. It is, after all, obedience required of *human* beings.

The Scheme
9:3-15

³But when the inhabitants of Gibeon heard what Joshua had done to Jericho and to Ai, ⁴they on their part acted with cunning, and went and made ready provisions,

and took worn-out sacks upon their asses, and wineskins, worn-out and torn and mended, [5]with worn-out, patched sandals on their feet, and worn-out clothes; and all their provisions were dry and moldy. [6]And they went to Joshua in the camp at Gilgal, and said to him and to the men of Israel, "We have come from a far country; so now make a covenant with us." [7]But the men of Israel said to the Hivites, "Perhaps you live among us; then how can we make a covenant with you?" [8]They said to Joshua, "We are your servants." And Joshua said to them, "Who are you? And where do you come from?" [9]They said to him, "From a very far country your servants have come, because of the name of the Lord your God; for we have heard a report of him, and all that he did in Egypt, [10]and all that he did to the two kings of the Amorites who were beyond the Jordan, Sihon the king of Heshbon, and Og king of Bashan, who dwelt in Ashtaroth. [11]And our elders and all the inhabitants of our country said to us, 'Take provisions in your hand for the journey, and go to meet them, and say to them, "We are your servants; come now, make a covenant with us." ' [12]Here is our bread; it was still warm when we took it from our houses as our food for the journey, on the day we set forth to come to you, but now, behold, it is dry and moldy; [13]these wineskins were new when we filled them, and behold, they are burst; and these garments and shoes of ours are worn out from the very long journey." [14]So the men partook of their provisions, and did not ask direction from the Lord. [15]And Joshua made peace with them, and made a covenant with them, to let them live; and the leaders of the congregation swore to them.

To avoid a bloody conflict with the Israelites over the possession of their land, the Gibeonites devise a scheme to trick Israel into making a peace treaty. The Gibeonites pretend to be from a distant land and therefore no threat to the Israelite tribes (vv. 6, 9). The Israelite tribes make a pact with the Gibeonites (v. 15). While the whole scene may appear to be quite improbable, it does preserve the memory of how the settlement proceeded at times in a peaceful manner. There was indeed some sort of an agreement between Israel and Gibeon since 2 Sam 21:1-14 assumes the existence of such a pact.

The scheme discovered
9:16-27

16At the end of three days after they had made a covenant with them, they heard that they were their neighbors, and that they dwelt among them. 17And the people of Israel set out and reached their cities on the third day. Now their cities were Gibeon, Chephirah, Beeroth, and Kiriath-jearim. 18But the people of Israel did not kill them, because the leaders of the congregation had sworn to them by the Lord, the God of Israel. Then all the congregation murmured against the leaders. 19But all the leaders said to all the congregation, "We have sworn to them by the Lord, the God of Israel, and now we may not touch them. 20This we will do to them, and let them live, lest wrath be upon us, because of the oath which we swore to them." 21And the leaders said to them, "Let them live." So they became hewers of wood and drawers of water for all the congregation, as the leaders had said of them.

22Joshua summoned them, and he said to them, "Why did you deceive us, saying, 'We are very far from you,' when you dwell among us? 23Now therefore you are cursed, and some of you shall always be slaves, hewers of wood and drawers of water for the house of my God." 24They answered Joshua, "Because it was told to your servants for a certainty that the Lord your God had commanded his servant Moses to give you all the land, and to destroy all the inhabitants of the land from before you; so we feared greatly for our lives because of you, and did this thing. 25And now, behold, we are in your hand: do as it seems good and right in your sight to do to us."

> [26]So he did to them, and delivered them out of the hand of the people of Israel; and they did not kill them. [27]But Joshua made them that day hewers of wood and drawers of water for the congregation and for the altar of the Lord, to continue to this day, in the place which he should choose.

It took the Israelites three days to discover that they had been tricked by the Gibeonites (v. 16), who readily admit their deception since they knew that Israel was bound to honor the pact between them (vv. 24-25). The Gibeonites' scheme was not entirely successful since they had to accept an inferior social status among the Israelite tribes (vv. 21, 23). Surely this detail is added here under the influence of Deut 29:11 which assumes that foreigners do not enjoy the same social status as Israelites.

The last half of v. 27 contains an anachronistic reference to the Jerusalem Temple. "The place which he should choose" is a variant of the standard formula by which Deuteronomy refers to Jerusalem (*cf.*, Deut 12). Certainly Joshua did not concern himself with providing servants for the cult. What is behind this brief allusion may be an attempt to explain why there have been non-Israelites in service at Israelite sanctuaries. The practice of using foreigners as temple slaves was common in the ancient Near East and may have survived in Judah to the time of Ezra (*cf.*, Ezra 8:17, 20; Neh 7:46-60).

THE CAMPAIGN SOUTH OF GIBEON
10:1-43

This chapter focuses on Joshua's conquests to the south of Gibeon. It is made up of three episodes and a concluding summary. The first two episodes (vv. 1-15: the defeat of the five-king coalition and vv. 16-27: the execution of the five kings) may be two independent traditions based on the same event: the victory of Israel over a Canaanite coalition. Verse 15 does point to the independence of these two traditions while Makkedah, a site mentioned in both episodes (vv. 10,

16), provides a convenient link between them. The defeat of
the Canaanite coalition opens up the entire south to Joshua
and a very brief description of his activity there makes up
the third episode (vv. 28-29). Finally vv. 40-43 summarize
the results of all Joshua's campaigns.

The Defeat of the Five-King Coalition
10:1-15

10 When Adonizedek king of Jerusalem heard how
Joshua had taken Ai, and had utterly destroyed it, doing
to Ai and its king as he had done to Jericho and its king,
and how the inhabitants of Gibeon had made peace with
Israel and were among them, ²he feared greatly, because
Gibeon was a great city, like one of the royal cities, and
because it was greater than Ai, and all its men were
mighty. ³So Adonizedek king of Jerusalem sent to
Hoham king of Hebron, to Piram king of Jarmuth, to
Japhia king of Lachish, and to Debir king of Eglon,
saying, ⁴"Come up to me, and help me, and let us smite
Gibeon; for it has made peace with Joshua and with the
people of Israel." ⁵Then the five kings of the Amorites,
the king of Jerusalem, the king of Hebron, the king of
Jarmuth, the king of Lachish, and the king of Eglon,
gathered their forces, and went up with all their armies
and encamped against Gibeon, and made war against it.

⁶And the men of Gibeon sent to Joshua at the camp in
Gilgal, saying 'Do not relax your hand from your servants; come up to us quickly, and save us, and help us; for
all the kings of the Amorites that dwell in the hill country
are gathered against us." ⁷So Joshua went up from Gilgal,
he and all the people of war with him, and all the mighty
men of valor. ⁸And the Lord said to Joshua, "Do not fear
them, for I have given them into your hands; there shall
not a man of them stand before you." ⁹So Joshua came
upon them suddenly, having marched up all night from
Gilgal. ¹⁰And the Lord threw them into a panic before
Israel, who slew them with a great slaughter at Gibeon,
and chased them by the way of the ascent of Beth-
horan, and smote them as far as Azekah and Makkedah. ¹¹And
as they fled before Israel, while they were going down the

ascent of Bethhoron, the Lord threw down great stones from heaven upon them as far as Azekah, and they died; there were more who died because of the hailstones than the men of Israel killed with the sword.

[12]Then spoke Joshua to the Lord in the day when the Lord gave the Amorites over to the men of Israel; and he said in the sight of Israel,

"Sun, stand thou still at Gibeon,
and thou Moon in the valley of Ai-jalon."

[13]And the sun stood still, and the moon stayed,
until the nation took vengeance on their enemies.

Is this not written in the Book of Jashar? The sun stayed in the midst of heaven, and did not hasten to go down for about a whole day. [14]There has been no day like it before or since, when the Lord hearkened to the voice of a man; for the Lord fought for Israel.

[15]Then Joshua returned, and all Israel with him, to the camp at Gilgal.

The treaty between Israel and Gibeon arouses the fears of a number of other Canaanite city-states which decide to move against Gibeon. The Gibeonites call upon their new allies for help. Joshua responds and the Canaanite coalition is defeated. These bare details of the story are quite plausible from a historical point of view. The text as it now stands describes the Israelite victory as aided by the Lord who miraculously intervenes in the course of the battle (vv. 11, 12-14). In fact, the Israelite victory over the five kings is presented as the outcome of a Holy War. God promised Israel complete victory (v. 8) and the rout of the Canaanite troops (v. 10-11) verifies this oracle of salvation. The account concludes with the observation that the "Lord fought for Israel" (v. 14).

The belief that the Lord fought for Israel is given graphic illustration through the mention of two miracles. The miracle of the hailstones (v. 11) is integrated into the prose account of the battle. The miracle of the sun (vv. 12-14) is recounted by means of a quotation from the poetry found in the Book of Jashar (the Righteous). This book, which has not survived, was apparently a text celebrating heroic achievements (*cf.,* 2 Sam 1:18). As a poetic celebration of the divine help given to Israel, vv. 12b-13 are similar to the Song of Moses (Exod 15) and the Song of Deborah (Judg 5). Recounting these miracles serves to reinforce the belief that Israel is invincible when God takes her side. According to the ideology of Holy War, it is God's might — not Israel's — which brings victory.

That Israel came to possess her territory in spite of Canaanite opposition is a historical reminiscence which is theologically significant to the Deuteronomistic author. That author was writing for the benefit of a nation whose future seemed to be determined by empires aligned against it. In reality, Israel's future will be determined by God. All Israel has to do to secure that future is to speak to God as Joshua did. "The Lord hearkened to the voice of a man" (v. 14) in the past, why not again?

Verse 15 has Joshua returning to Gilgal at the conclusion of his successful campaign against the Canaanite coalition. The following verse has Joshua pursuing the five kings who obviously survived the defeat of their forces. The Septuagint omits v. 15 to clear up this discrepancy. Obviously there are two originally independent traditions here which only later came to be associated with one another. It is quite likely that these two independent traditions are both based on the memory of the same event: the defeat of the Canaanite coalition.

Over the years two passages from the Book of Joshua have captured the popular imagination. The first is the passage describing how Jericho's walls "came a tumblin' down" (6:15-27). The other is the story of the sun's "standing still" at Joshua's request (10:12-14). Similar occurrences have been described in other texts from antiquity, and our scientific age has come up with a list of astronomical "explanations" of the phenomenon alluded to here. There is even the suggestion that this text alludes to the best time for military attack: the pre-dawn hours before the setting of the moon in the west and the rising of the sun in the east! In all probability these verses are modeled after ancient Near Eastern pre-battle incantations which regarded the simultaneous appearance of the sun and the moon in the morning sky as a favorable omen. Whatever the origin of this brief quotation from the Book of the Righteous, the Deuteronomist cites it as a testimony to the power of God who fights Israel's battles. What Joshua does best is to pray! What the Exiles need to do is to imitate Joshua.

The Execution of the Five Kings
10:16-27

16These five kings fled, and hid themselves in the cave at Makkedah. 17And it was told Joshua, "The five kings have been found, hidden in the cave at Makkedah." 18And Joshua said, "Roll great stones against the mouth of the cave, and set men by it to guard them; 19but do not stay there yourselves, pursue your enemies, fall upon their rear, do not let them enter their cities; for the Lord your God has given them into your hand." 20When Joshua and the men of Israel had finished slaying them with a very great slaughter, until they were wiped out, and when the remnant which remained of them had entered into the fortified cities, 21all the people returned safe to Joshua in the camp at Makkedah; not a man moved his tongue against any of the people of Israel.

22Then Joshua said, "Open the mouth of the cave, and bring those five kings out to me from the cave." 23And they did so, and brought those five kings out to him from the cave, the king of Jerusalem, the king of Hebron, the king of Jarmuth, the king of Lachish, and the king of Eglon. 24And when they brought those kings out to Joshua, Joshua summoned all the men of Israel, and said to the chiefs of the men of war who had gone with him, "Come near, put your feet upon the necks of these kings." Then they came near, and put their feet on their necks.

25And Joshua said to them, "Do not be afraid or dismayed; be strong and of good courage; for thus the Lord will do to all your enemies against whom you fight." 26And afterward Joshua smote them and put them to death, and he hung them on five trees. And they hung upon the trees until evening; 27but at the time of the going down of the sun, Joshua commanded, and they took them down from the trees, and threw them into the cave where they had hidden themselves, and they set great stones against the mouth of the cave, which remain to this very day.

Though the kings had well-fortified cities of their own within which to seek refuge, this passage would have us believe that the five kings hid in a cave. Clearly then this text is a popular etiological tradition connected with the cave and large stones near Makkedah. Though the form of the story as it now stands may be popular legend, it nonetheless may have a genuine historical basis which is the same as that for the previous story: the victory of Israel over a Canaanite coalition. In addition elements of Holy War ideology have been introduced to the story (vv. 19, 25). Israel is not to fear since God has given assurance of victory.

The Southern Campaign
10:28-39

28And Joshua took Makkedah on that day, and smote it and its king with the edge of the sword; he utterly destroyed every person in it, he left none remaining; and he did to the king of Makkedah as he had done to the king of Jericho.

29Then Joshua passed on from Makkedah, and all Israel with him, to Libnah, and fought against Libnah; 30and the Lord gave it also and its king into the hand of Israel; and he smote it with the edge of the sword, and every person in it; he left none remaining in it; and he did to its king as he had done to the king of Jericho.

31And Joshua passed on from Libnah, and all Israel

with him, to Lachish, and laid seige to it, and assaulted it: [32]and the Lord gave Lachish into the hand of Israel, and he took it on the second day, and smote it with the edge of the sword, and every person in it, as he had done to Libnah.

[33]Then Horam king of Gezer came up to help Lachish; and Joshua smote him and his people, until he left none remaining.

[34]And Joshua passed on with all Israel from Lachish to Eglon; and they laid seige to it, and assaulted it; [35]and they took it on that day, and smote it with the edge of the sword; and every person in it he utterly destroyed that day, as he had done to Lachish.

[36]Then Joshua went up with all Israel from Eglon to Hebron; and they assaulted it, [37]and took it, and smote it with the edge of the sword, and its king and its towns, and every person in it; he left none remaining, as he had done to Eglon, and utterly destroyed it with every person in it.

[38]Then Joshua, with all Israel, turned back to Debir and assaulted it, [39]and he took it with its king and all its towns; and they smote them with the edge of the sword, and utterly destroyed every person in it; he left none remaining; as he had done to Hebron and to Libnah and its king, so he did to Debir and to its king.

Only a few details are given of the remainder of Joshua's southern campaign. Even these scanty details cause some problems since they stand in conflict with Josh 14:6-15; 15:13-19 and Judg 1:11-21, which credit Caleb with the victories over Hebron and Debir. Apparently this passage was composed by someone familiar with the extent of the Davidic-Solomonic empire in the southern regions of Palestine. Joshua is simply credited with acquiring that territory for Israel. Archaeology provides no clear evidence of an Israelite conquest of this territory in the 13th century B.C. In view of these difficulties it is unlikely that these verses provide a historical guide to what actually occurred during the period of the Israelite settlement. They represent rather the conviction that Canaan was acquired by an armed conflict with the indigenous population. Joshua provides the leadership for the Israelite tribes during this conflict. As a result, the acquisition of all territories, even at a later period of time, is credited to Joshua.

A Summary
10:40-43

40So Joshua defeated the whole land, the hill country and the Negeb and the lowland and the slopes, and all their kings; he left none remaining, but utterly destroyed all that breathed, as the Lord God of Israel commanded. 41And Joshua defeated them from Kadeshbarnea to Gaza, and all the country of Goshen, as far as Gibeon. 42And Joshua took all these kings and their land at one time, because the Lord God of Israel fought for Israel. 43Then Joshua returned, and all Israel with him, to the camp at Gilgal.

This summary indicates that Joshua completed the conquest of "the whole land" (v. 40). This may indicate that the following chapter was added to an already existing account of the conquest which concluded with chapter 10.

The Northern Campaign
11:1-15

11 When Jabin king of Hazor heard of this, he sent to Jobab king of Madon, and to the king of Shimron, and to the king of Achshaph, 2and to the kings who were in the northern hill country, and in the Arabah south of Chinneroth, and in the lowland, and in Naphothdor on the west, 3to the Canaanites in the east and the west, the Amorites, the Hittites, the Perizzites, and the Jebusites in the hill country, and the Hivites under Hermon in the land of

Mizpah. [4]And they came out, with all their troops, a great host, in number like the sand that is upon the seashore, with very many horses and chariots. [5]And all these kings joined their forces, and came and encamped together at the waters of Merom, to fight with Israel.

[6]And the Lord said to Joshua, "Do not be afraid of them, for tomorrow at this time I will give over all of them, slain, to Israel; you shall hamstring their horses, and burn their chariots with fire." [7]So Joshua came suddenly upon them with all his people of war, by the waters of Merom, and fell upon them. [8]And the Lord gave them into the hand of Israel, who smote them and chased them as far as Great Sidon and Misrephothmaim, and eastward as far as the valley of Mizpeh; and they smote them, until they left none remaining. [9]And Joshua did to them as the Lord bade him; he hamstrung their horses, and burned their chariots with fire.

[10]And Joshua turned back at that time, and took Hazor, and smote its king with the sword; for Hazor formerly was the head of all those kingdoms. [11]And they put to the sword all who were in it, utterly destroying them; there was none left that breathed, and he burned Hazor with fire. [12]And all the cities of those kings, and all their kings, Joshua took, and smote them with the edge of the sword, utterly destroying them, as Moses the servant of the Lord had commanded. [13]But none of the cities that stood on mounds did Israel burn, except Hazor only; that Joshua burned. [14]And all the spoil of these cities and the cattle, the people of Israel took for their booty; but every man they smote with the edge of the sword, until they had destroyed them, and they did not leave any that breathed. [15]As the Lord had commanded Moses his servant, so Moses commanded Joshua, and so Joshua did; he left nothing undone of all that the Lord had commanded Moses.

The provenance of this story of Israel's victories in the north is unlike that of some of the other narratives connected with the settlement. Some of these were connected with Israelite sanctuaries, *e.g.,* the story of the Jordan River crossing was associated with Gilgal and its memorial stones (4:19-24). Others were connected with famous landmarks, *i.e.,* the story of Ai was associated with the famous ruins near Bethel (8:28). The story of Joshua's victory over Jabin and his coalition makes no etiological allusions that reflect such associations. The origins of this narrative are to be located in the memory of those tribes which began to make incursions into the fertile areas of Galilee. Settlement there could have been intensive and made possible economic ties with the Phoenician coast. This account of Israel's encounter with another Canaanite coalition shows that this incursion did not take place peacefully. The Israelite tribes had to wrest control of this territory from the Canaanite city states, the most important of which was Hazor.

Hazor's dominant position in the north was due to its situation on important trade routes. While it was inhabited since the 3rd millennium B.C., Hazor flourished from 1800 B.C. until its destruction during the middle of the 13th century B.C., the period of the Israelite conquest. Archaeological evidence even supports the narrative when it says that Hazor was destroyed by fire. In addition, evaluation of relevant historical data indicates that the Israelite tribes are the most likely candidates for the responsibility of destroying this city.

While the Israelite tribes did take and raze Hazor, it was no easy task. Excavations have shown Hazor to be a very large and well fortified city. Its 190 acres make it by far the largest city of ancient Palestine. This text does not provide much information on how Israel managed to take Hazor. The parallels between this text and the previous chapter indicate that the victory in the north is being presented in fairly stereotyped fashion. A coalition formed by a king of an important Canaanite city-state attempts to turn back the Israelite tribes. After taking the initiative, Joshua wins a decisive victory over the coalition. Additional military activity allows Israel to consolidate the effects of its victory.

Of course, divine help is decisive in Israel's triumphs (10:8; 11:6).

This emphasis on divine help naturally suppresses any direct information on precisely how Israel achieved her victory. The decisive battle at Merom is not described nor is any seige of Hazor indicated. Were it possible to locate the "waters of Merom" with precision, perhaps some inferences could be made. If the battle took place near the present-day town of Meiron, the terrain would have rendered the chariots of the coalition practically useless. A surprise attack there (v. 7) would have enabled the Israelite forces to neutralize Hazor's principal defense. In such circumstances, Hazor's fall to the Israelite armies is quite understandable.

The silence on the military aspects of the victory is a consequence of the Deuteronomist's intention to underscore what he believes to be the real reason for Israel's triumph over Jabin: obedience to the Lord's commands (v. 15). The formidable list of Israel's enemies (v. 3), the description of the size and equipment of their combined armies (v. 4) and their clear intention to march against Israel (v. 5) are all intended to emphasize the impossible situation in which Israel found herself. The specific mention of the coalition's chariot forces heightens the sense of Israel's desperation since she always had special difficulties with chariotry (Josh 17:16-18; Judg 1:19; 4:13).

While no details of the actual battles at Merom or Hazor are given, there is a clear stress upon the divine assistance first promised (v. 6) and later given (v. 8) to Israel. The Lord saved Israel from the impossible situation in which she found herself. The conflict with the northern Canaanite coalition was brought to a successful conclusion not so much because of Joshua's military tactics but principally because of his obedience to the Lord's commands (v. 15). From the Deuteronomist's point of view, Joshua still provides Judah with the same type of leadership. If God's people will follow Joshua's example and leave "nothing undone of all that the Lord commanded Moses," the Lord would once again save them from the impossible situation which they faced: the Exile.

A Summary of Israel's Victories
11:16-23

16So Joshua took all that land, the hill country and all the Negeb and all the land of Goshen and the lowland and the Arabah and the hill country of Israel and its lowland 17from Mount Halak, that rises toward Seir, as far as Baalgad in the valley of Lebanon below Mount Hermon. And he took all their kings, and smote them, and put them to death. 18Joshua made war a long time with all those kings. 19There was not a city that made peace with the people of Israel, except the Hivites, the inhabitants of Gibeon; they took all in battle. 20For it was the Lord's doing to harden their hearts that they should come against Israel in battle, in order that they should be utterly destroyed, and should receive no mercy but be exterminated, as the Lord commanded Moses.

21And Joshua came at that time, and wiped out the Anakim from the hill country, from Hebron, from Debir, from Anab, and from all the hill country of Judah, and from all the hill country of Israel; Joshua utterly destroyed them with their cities. 22There was none of the Anakim left in the land of the people of Israel; only in Gaza, in Gath, and in Ashdod, did some remain. 23So Joshua took the whole land, according to all that the Lord had spoken to Moses; and Joshua gave it for an inheritance to Israel according to their tribal allotments. And the land had rest from war.

This programmatic summary of Israel's victories in Canaan contains an apologetic for Israel's treatment of the indigenous Canaanite population. This apologetic makes use of the "hardened heart" motif (v. 20). This same motif was used to explain Israel's confrontation with Egypt (Exod 4:21 *et passim*). The belief at the basis of this motif was that sins can be so great that God must step in and insure that retribution cannot be avoided. This is accomplished when God "hardens the heart" of the sinners to eliminate the possibility of their repentance. In the case of the Canaanites Israel becomes the means whereby this retribution takes place: "...because of these abominable practices the Lord your God is driving them out before you" (Deut 18:12b). From the perspective of the Deuteronomist, this same pattern has been repeated in Israel's life. Her disobedience became so pervasive that God's pardon was precluded and Israel had to be given over to the power of Babylon, the Lord's chosen instrument of retribution (2 Kgs 24:5, 20). The great irony here is that what has happened to the Canaanites is going to happen to Israel!

Under the leadership of Joshua, however, Israel did remain faithful to Yahweh and thus was always victorious — even over the dreaded Anakim (v. 22, *cf.,* Deut 2:10-11; Josh 13:12). All that remains is for the apportionment of the land among the tribes (v. 23). It is significant that this summary concludes with the note that the land had "rest" from war (v. 23). The word used for rest here is the one found frequently in Judges (3:11, 31; 5:31; 8:28 *et passim*). This may indicate that this rest is only temporary — a subtle hint of Israel's future inconstancy.

The Distribution of the Land
12:1-19:51

The text of Josh 12-19 will not be reproduced here. Chapter 12 is another summary of Israel's victories in Canaan. Both the victories of Moses in Transjordan (vv. 1-6) and those of Joshua in Cisjordan (vv. 7-24) are merely listed with no elaboration. Many of these latter victories are not described at all in Joshua.

Chapters 13-21 are entirely devoted to describing the distribution of the land. This distribution begins even though not all territories have been acquired from their previous inhabitants (13:2-7). Most of the "unconquered" land, however, lies outside of Palestine proper. While all the geographical data provided by these chapters is not entirely clear and consistent, it is possible to have a general idea of the tribal allotments. See the map on p. 78 for details.

At this point, it is appropriate to consider the attempts that have been made to provide an historical reconstruction of how the Israelite tribes did acquire Canaan. As we have seen, the Biblical and archaeological data is not entirely consistent and reconcilable. There are basically three approaches to the reconstruction of the conquest period. What follows is a brief description of each.

The Invasion Model

The invasion model presents the twelve tribes as invading Canaan from Transjordan toward the end of the 13th century B.C. The tribes engaged in a concerted effort aimed at the total destruction of the populace of Canaan. The Israelite conquest is completed in the space of a few years with an initial campaign in central Canaan followed by later campaigns in the South and then in the North. The conquest ends with the tribes dividing the conquered lands among themselves.

While this model proports to be based on both the Biblical narrative and archaeological data, closer examination of both does call this assertion into question. First of all, the Biblical data actually describes battles in rather limited areas of Canaan. Israelite victories are clustered in the territory of Benjamin (Josh 6, 8, 9), Judah (10) and Naphtali (11). As a result of a more perceptive reading of the conquest narratives, the invasion model has been modified by some who propose an invasion by just a few tribes under the leadership of Joshua whose campaigns break the back of Canaanite opposition and make possible later consolidation of the rest of Canaan without serious opposition.

Secondly the weight of archaeological data seems to contradict rather than support the invasion model. Though some cities in Palestine were destroyed in the 13th century B.C., these do not always include those mentioned in the text. For example, at that time Jericho was nothing more than an unwalled settlement (compare Josh 6). In addition,

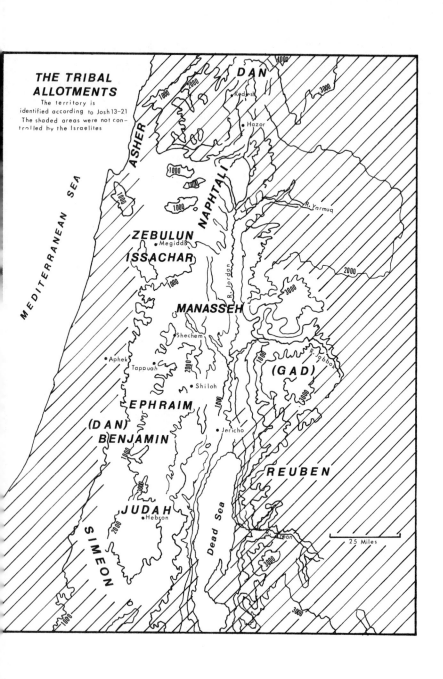

THE TRIBAL
ALLOTMENTS
The territory is
identified according to Josh 13-21
The shaded areas were not con-
trolled by the Israelites

MEDITERRANEAN SEA

ASHER

DAN

• Kedesh

• Hazor

1000
2000
3000
4000

R. Yarmuq

NAPHTALI

1000

ZEBULUN
• Megiddo

ISSACHAR

2000

1000

R. Jordan

3000

MANASSEH

• Shechem

• Aphek

Tappuah •

2000

• Shiloh

(GAD)

R. Jabbok

1000

3000

EPHRAIM

(DAN)

BENJAMIN

1000

• Jericho

REUBEN

JUDAH

• Hebron

2000

Dead Sea

R. Arnon

25 Miles

SIMEON

1000

2000

3000

there is no way of determining that any destruction that did take place was actually the work of Israelite invaders. While the Biblical and archaeological data do point to the destruction of some Canaanite cities in the late 13th century B.C., this data has not been successfully extrapolated into supporting the invasion model.

The Immigration Model

In direct opposition to the invasion model is the immigration model which describes the land-taking by the Israelite tribes as the result of a series of uncoordinated movements into Canaan by Israelites from the patriarchal period up to the time of David. The Canaanites were never really annihilated by the incoming Israelites since conflicts between the two groups occurred only sporadically. The immigrating Israelites usually managed to live peaceably with the Canaanites until the time of David. David's absorption of the Canaanites into his empire caused a cultural and religious struggle which continued throughout the period of the monarchy. The story of the conquest with its description of Joshua's conflicts with and victories over the Canaanites was simply a propaganda tool in the hands of Yahwists who objected to the syncretist tendencies of some in monarchic Israel.

The principal objections to the immigration model are that it minimizes the value of archaeology in the historical reconstruction of this period of Israel's life and that it is quite selective in its reading of the Biblical material. A serious weakness of this model is that it offers no plausible explanation of Israel's unity given the fragmented and uncoordinated beginning it posits for the tribes.

The Revolt Model

A third approach is provided by the revolt model which posits that Israel was made up of a considerable number of native Canaanites who revolted against their political leaders by joining forces with an invading group from Transjordan (the Israelite Exodus group). This model interprets the available Biblical and archaeological evidence from the perspective of anthropology and sociology. It takes into account the socio-economic and political situation of 13th century Canaan and concludes that this area was ripe for revolt. The Amarna Letters sent by Canaanite vassals to their Egyptian overlords a century earlier describe considerable unrest among the populace. Yahwism then provided the spark that ignited the movement of the marginalized elements of Canaan's citizens against an unjust and repressive social system.

This approach has the advantage of being more flexible in its ability to make úse of available archaeological and Biblical data. For example, the destruction of sites in Canaan can be ascribed to agencies other than the invading Exodus group under the leadership of Joshua. Secondly, even though the Biblical narrative may emphasize the unity of the tribes, the revolt model can help discover evidence of a more diverse origin for the Israelite tribes. For example, Josh 24 can be seen as the incorporation into Israel of a significant portion of the native Canaanite population.

Objections to this model center on its inability to present well developed Biblical evidence in support of its thesis. The Bible does attempt to portray the conquest as an all-Israel affair directed against the Canaanites. Secondly the revolt model has been criticized as a retrojection of modern views on social revolution upon a situation from antiquity. Any evidence for a "revolt" is seen less as a consequence of Biblical data correctly interpreted and more as a projection of the socio-economic views of the interpreter.

While discussion continues with regard to an appropriate model for the historical reconstruction of the Israelite conquest of Canaan, it is clear that new political and sociological analysis will have to be components of any future model. Dependence solely upon literary analysis and interpretation of archaeological data along "traditional" lines is no longer acceptable. Yahwism has been shown to be not only a religious and cultural phenomenon; it was a socio-economic and political force as well. One cannot ignore this reality while attempting to determine how Israel acquired the land which was to be the scene of her subsequent history.

The Cities of Asylum
20:1-9

20 Then the Lord said to Joshua, [2]"Say to the people of Israel, 'Appoint the cities of refuge, of which I spoke to you through Moses, [3]that the manslayer who kills any person without intent or unwittingly may flee there; they shall be for you a refuge from the avenger of blood. [4]He shall flee to one of these cities and shall stand at the entrance of the gate of the city, and explain his case to the elders of that city; then they shall take him into the city, and give him a place, and he shall remain with them. [5]And if the avenger of blood pursues him, they shall not give up the slayer into his hand; because he killed his neighbor unwittingly, having had no enmity against him in times past. [6]And he shall remain in that city until he has stood before the congregation for judgment, until the death of him who is high priest at the time: then the slayer may go again to his own town and his own home, to the town from which he fled.'"

[7]So they set apart Kedesh in Galilee in the hill country of Naphtali and Shechem in the hill country of Ephraim, and Kiriatharba (that is, Hebron) in the hill country of Judah. [8]And beyond the Jordan east of Jericho, they appointed Bezer in the wilderness on the tableland, from the tribe of Reuben, and Ramoth in Gilead, from the tribe of Gad, and Golan in Bashan, from the tribe of Manasseh. [9]These were the cities designated for all the people of Israel, and for the stranger sojourning among them, that any one who killed a person without intent could flee there, so that he might not die by the hand of the avenger of blood, till he stood before the congregation.

In the course of the allotment of Canaanite territory among the tribes, the Lord reminds Joshua of the Deuteronomic precept regarding cities of asylum (Deut 19:1-13). This law provides for places of refuge to protect those involved in accidental homicide (v. 3). Without such places of asylum, the one responsible for the accident would be sought out and killed by the deceased individual's kin (v. 5). This act of revenge would inspire another until the cycle of blood vengeance would threaten the very fabric of society. In the ancient Near East generally, blood vengeance was ruled out as socially unacceptable long before the emergence of the Israelite tribes. In its place, the injured family was to approach the sovereign for redress. Since the Israelite tribes had no sovereign, another approach had to be taken in order to prevent blood vengeance from reasserting itself. The cities of refuge were a distinctive Israelite institution which attempted to replace blood vengeance with a more reasoned and calm approach in dealing with accidental homicide. Six cities were set apart: three in Cisjordan (v. 7) and three in Transjordan (v. 8).

Unfortunately no Biblical text gives a specific example of how this institution actually functioned. The allusion to the death of the high priest (v. 6) is a particular problem. The high priest is not mentioned in the Deuteronomic law but is part of the Priestly version of this legislation (Num 35:28). According to this priestly legislation, the one responsible for the accidental homicide must remain in the city of refuge until the death of the high priest or else place himself in danger of blood vengeance. The Deuteronomic law has the individual remain in the city of refuge only until the elders determine that the homicide was indeed accidental.

The Levitical Cities
21:1-3

21   Then the heads of the fathers' houses of the Levites came to Eleazar the priest and to Joshua the son of Nun and to the heads of the fathers' houses of the tribes of the people of Israel; ²and they said to them at Shiloh in the land of Canaan, "The Lord commanded through Moses that we be given cities to dwell in, along with their pasture lands for our cattle." ³So by command of the Lord the people of Israel gave to the Levites the following cities and pasture lands out of their inheritance.

The command of the Lord which vv. 2-3 refer to is probably Num 35:1-8. In reality, however, the Numbers text is dependent upon Josh 21:1-42 since it assumes that the cities of asylum will be among the Levitical cities (Num 35:6) while this detail is only secondarily inserted into Josh 21.

This chapter preserves the memory that Levi was a special case among the tribes. For some reason it was never able to acquire and maintain its own territory. The landless Levites turned to the cult for support and soon became the preferred cultic functionaries in Israel (*cf.*, Judg 17-18). Deuteronomy assumes that the Levites who were able to continue functioning as priests will find their support from that service (Deut 18:1-8); otherwise, that book commends the members of this landless tribe to the charity of their fellow Israelites (*cf.*, Deut 12:12; 14:27-29). There is no provision in Deuteronomy for any "Levitical cities."

As in the case with the cities of asylum, the Biblical text offers no concrete example of the way this institution may have functioned. Were these Levitical cities established to provide the Levites with an income? Were they places where those who wished to retain their Levitical identity settled? That there were places where Levitical families lived together is about all that can be safely inferred from this text.

Josh 21:4-21 will not be reproduced here. These verses record the assignment of various cities to the Levitical families. This list of cities is not without problems. Some of these cities were not taken by Israel until the Davidic-Solomonic period (*e.g.*, Gezer and Taanach). Others, especially in the Transjordan region, were abandoned after the time of Solomon.

A Summary
21:43-45

> [43]Thus the Lord gave to Israel all the land which he swore to give to their fathers; and having taken possession of it, they settled there. [44]And the Lord gave them rest on every side just as he had sworn to their fathers; not one of all their enemies had withstood them, for the Lord had given all their enemies into their hands. [45]Not one of all the good promises which the Lord had made to the house of Israel had failed; all came to pass.

This passage is a programmatic summary of the Israelite settlement of Canaan: v. 43 describes the distribution of the land, v. 44 describes the conquest and v. 45 characterizes the entry and occupation of Canaan as complete and final. All the promises have been fulfilled.

This summary assumes the complete annihilation of the indigenous Canaanite population (10:40-43; 11:16-20, 23). Yahweh is the one who fights for Israel and defeats her enemies. Israel's entry into Canaan is seen as a single, concerted invasion leading to a complete victory with the result that Israel enjoys "rest on every side" (v. 44). In short, this passage is an early etiology of Israel's being in Canaan.

The passage of time modified the views reflected in this text. Under the influence of the Book of Deuteronomy, Israel's possession of the land came to be seen not as a once-and-for-all event but as conditioned on her obedience. In Josh 23 this changed perspective will become apparent. The "rest" of Josh 23:1 is not forever since disobedience can cause Israel to "perish from this good land" (23:13).

The Dismissal of the Transjordan Tribes
22:1-9

22 Then Joshua summoned the Reubenites, and the Gadites, and the half-tribe of Manasseh, [2]and said to them, "You have kept all that Moses the servant of the Lord commanded you, and have obeyed my voice in all that I have commanded you; ³you have not forsaken your brethren these many days, down to this day, but have been careful to keep the charge of the Lord your God. ⁴And now the Lord your God has given rest to your brethren, as he promised them; therefore turn and go to your home in the land where your possession lies, which Moses the servant of the Lord gave you on the other side of the Jordan. ⁵Take good care to observe the commandment and the law which Moses the servant of the Lord commanded you, to love the Lord your God, and to walk in all his ways, and to keep his commandments, and to cleave to him, and to serve him with all your heart and with all your soul." ⁶So Joshua blessed them, and sent them away; and they went to their homes.

⁷Now to the one half of the tribe of Manasseh Moses had given a possession in Bashan; but to the other half Joshua had given a possession beside their brethren in the land west of the Jordan. And when Joshua sent them away to their homes and blessed them, ⁸he said to them, "Go back to your homes with much wealth, and with very many cattle, with silver, gold, bronze, and iron, and with much clothing; divide the spoil of your enemies with your brethren." ⁹So the Reubenites and the Gadites and the half-tribe of Manasseh returned home, parting from the people of Israel at Shiloh, which is in the land of Canaan, to go to the land of Gilead, their own land of which they had possessed themselves by command of the Lord through Moses.

These verses are actually a Deuteronomistic preamble to the story regarding the controversy over the altar in the Jordan valley (vv. 10-34). The tribes of Reuben, Gad and the eastern part of Manasseh are permitted to return to their own territories since the purpose for their presence in Cis-jordan has been accomplished: the other tribes now have their land and enjoy rest from the Lord (v. 4). What was begun with Joshua's address to these tribes in 1:12-18 is now brought to completion. The tribes are dismissed in typically Deuteronomic fashion — with the admonition to observe "the commandment and law" of Moses (v. 5).

A Conflict Over Altars
22:10-34

¹⁰And when they came to the region about the Jordan, that lies in the land of Canaan, the Reubenites and the Gadites and the half-tribe of Manasseh built there an altar by the Jordan, an altar of great size. ¹¹And the people of Israel heard say, "Behold, the Reubenites and the Gadites and the half-tribe of Manasseh have built an altar at the frontier of the land of Canaan, in the region about the Jordan, on the side that belongs to the people of Israel." ¹²And when the people of Israel heard of it, the whole assembly of the people of Israel gathered at Shiloh, to make war against them.

¹³Then the people of Israel sent to the Reubenites and the Gadites and the half-tribe of Manasseh, in the land of Gilead, Phinehas the son of Eleazar the priest, ¹⁴and with him ten chiefs, one from each of the tribal families of Israel, every one of them the head of a family among the clans of Israel. ¹⁵And they came to the Reubenites, the Gadites and the half-tribe of Manasseh, in the land of Gilead, and they said to them, ¹⁶"Thus says the whole congregation of the Lord, 'What is this treachery which you have committed against the God of Israel in turning away this day from following the Lord, by building yourselves an altar this day in rebellion against the Lord? ¹⁷Have we not had enough of the sin at Peor from which even yet we have not cleansed ourselves, and for which there came a plague upon the congregation of the Lord, ¹⁸that you must turn away this day from following the Lord? And if you rebel against the Lord today he will be angry with the whole congregation of Israel tomorrow.

¹⁹But now, if your land is unclean, pass over into the Lord's land where the Lord's tabernacle stands, and take for yourselves a possession among us; only do not rebel against the Lord, or make us as rebels by building yourselves an altar other than the altar of the Lord our God. ²⁰Did not Achan the son of Zerah break faith in the matter of the devoted things, and wrath fell upon all the congregation of Israel? And he did not perish alone for his iniquity.'"

²¹Then the Reubenites, the Gadites, and the half-tribe of Manasseh said in answer to the heads of the families of Israel, ²²"The Mighty One, God, the Lord! The Mighty One, God, the Lord! He knows; and let Israel itself know! If it was in rebellion or in breach of faith toward the Lord, spare us not today ²³for building an altar to turn away from following the Lord; or if we did so to offer burnt offerings or cereal offerings or peace offerings on it, may the Lord himself take vengeance. ²⁴Nay, but we did it from fear that in time to come your children might say to our children, 'What have you to do with the Lord, the God of Israel? ²⁵For the Lord has made the Jordan a boundary between us and you, you Reubenites and Gadites; you have no portion in the Lord.' So your children might make our children cease to worship the Lord. ²⁶Therefore we said, 'Let us now build an altar, not for burnt offering, nor for sacrifice, ²⁷but to be a witness between us and you, and between the generations after us, that we do perform the service of the Lord in his presence with our burnt offerings and sacrifices and peace offerings; lest your children say to our children in time to come, "You have no portion in the Lord." '²⁸And we thought, If this should be said to us or our descendants in time to come, we should say, 'Behold the copy of the altar of the Lord, which our fathers made, not for burnt offerings, nor for sacrifice, but to be a witness between us and you.' ²⁹Far be it from us that we should rebel against the Lord, and turn away this day from following the Lord by building an altar for burnt offer-

ing, cereal offering, or sacrifice, other than the altar of the Lord our God that stands before his tabernacle!"

[30]When Phinehas the priest and the chiefs of the congregation, the heads of the families of Israel who were with him, heard the words that the Reubenites and the Gadites and the Manassites spoke, it pleased them well. [31]And Phinehas the son of Eleazar the priest said to the Reubenites and the Gadites and the Manassites, "Today, we know that the Lord is in the midst of us, because you have not committed this treachery against the Lord; now you have saved the people of Israel from the hand of the Lord."

[32]Then Phinehas the son of Eleazar the priest, and the chiefs, returned from the Reubenites and the Gadites in the land of Gilead to the land of Canaan, to the people of Israel, and brought back word to them. [33]And the report pleased the people of Israel; and the people of Israel blessed God and spoke no more of making war against them, to destroy the land where the Reubenites and the Gadites were settled. [34]The Reubenites and the Gadites called the altar Witness; "For," said they, "it is a witness between us that the Lord is God."

According to Num 32:5, the Transjordan tribes ask to be allowed not to cross the Jordan. These two tribes play no part in the narratives about the conquest of Canaan of Josh 1-11 and Judg 1. Their participation in the conquest is expressed, however, in Josh 1:12-18 and 22:1-9 both of which are late Deuteronomistic texts. Both texts attempt to portray the conquest of Canaan as an all-Israel affair. More than likely, the Israelites of the Transjordan did not participate in battles outside their own territory and this caused a certain amount of friction between them and the Israelites of the Cisjordan. This text reflects one instance of that friction.

In the situation narrated here, the particular cause for the flare-up of friction was a conflict between two rival sanctuaries. Though this narrative does not supply all the details, this rivalry was probably between the sanctuary at Gilgal which was very near the Jordan and that of Shiloh which was in the center of the Ephraimite hill country. Of course, the Transjordan tribes would have favored Gilgal since it was in close proximity to their own territory. In fact, they argue that it was necessary in order to preserve their identity as worshippers of Yahweh (vv. 24-25). The more distant shrine at Shiloh could not insure this as effectively. How this conflict was settled cannot be determined with any certainty, but both Gilgal and Shiloh remained tribal sanctuaries. The latter was probably destroyed by the Philistines in the middle of the 11th century B.C. (*cf.,* Jer 7:12, 14; 26:6, 9), while the former went on to be one of the great shrines of the Northern Kingdom (Am 4:4; 5:5; Hos 9:15; 12:12).

The remnants of this old tradition concerning the rivalry between Gilgal and Shiloh were reworked by the Deuteronomist as an example story illustrating the law of centralization (*cf.,* Deut 12). Even in the tribal era, this law was being observed. The Deuteronomist has the Transjordan tribes recognizing the validity of the law requiring a single sanctuary and declaring that their altar is not a true altar but only a "witness" of their adherence to the worship of Yahweh (vv. 24-29). The detail about the size of the altar (v. 10), however, does indicate that it was indeed an altar of sacrifice. An altar of "great size" which at the same time was not an altar is incongruous.

Some of the vocabulary in this passage points to redaction by the author of the Priestly History of Israel (P). Since the priest Phinehas rather than Joshua plays a prominent part here (vv. 13, 30-32), redaction by P is likely. Nonetheless the principal reactional work was done by the Deuteronomist who uses an ancient tradition about rivalry between the tribes as his first opportunity to introduce the "single sanctuary" motif which is so critical to Deuteronomic theology.

Joshua's Farewell to Israel
23:1-16

The Book of Joshua closes with two chapters whose hortatory emphasis is clear. Together with chapter one,

Josh 23 and 24 frame the book and underscore its intended purpose: to encourage Israel to be obedient to the conditions of the covenant as they find expression in the book of the law (1:8; 23:6; 24:26). While Josh 24 emphasizes the Lord's actions in the past as a stimulus to fidelity, Josh 23 focuses on what the Lord will do in the future if Israel choses the path of infidelity.

The vocabulary and style of Josh 23 is reminiscent of the Book of Deuteronomy. One feature of that style is repetition. Three elements surface a number of times in this chapter: a reminder of what the Lord has done for Israel (vv. 3, 9, 14b-15a), an exhortation to obedience (vv. 6-8, 11) and threats upon an unfaithful Israel (vv. 12-13, 15b-16). The function of this repetitious style is to emphasize one central idea: obedience brings blessing while disobedience brings a curse. This is a fundamental Deuteronomic understanding of how the Law of God operates: it can be a blessing or a curse (*cf.*, Deut 30:15-20).

No locality is specified for Joshua's farewell address. This indeterminate locality plus the fact that Joshua addresses "all Israel" indicate that the message Joshua delivers is not bound to any one place or time. Its theme, the conditional nature of the covenant, is a message that all Israel needs to hear at every moment of her life. In other words, the choices that Israel had to make at the conclusion of Joshua's life are the same type of choices that Israel continued to face throughout her life in the land and which the Exiles now face as they hope for Israel's restoration. In a sense Israel determines her future by the choices she makes with regard to the conditions of her covenant with the Lord.

THE COVENANT IS CONDITIONAL
23:1-13

23   A long time afterward, when the Lord had given rest to Israel from all their enemies round about, and Joshua was old and well advanced in years, ²Joshua summoned all Israel, their elders and heads, their judges and officers, and said to them, "I am now old and well advanced in years; ³and you have seen all that the Lord your God has done to all these nations for your sake, for it is the Lord your God who has fought for you. ⁴Behold, I have allotted to you as an inheritance for your tribes those nations that remain, along with all the nations that I already cut off, from the Jordan to the Great Sea in the west. ⁵The Lord your God will push them back before you, and drive them out of your sight; and you shall possess their land, as the Lord your God promised you. ⁶Therefore be very steadfast to keep and do all that is written in the book of the law of Moses, turning aside from it neither to the right hand nor to the left, ⁷that you may not be mixed with these nations left here among you, or make mention of the names of their gods, or swear by them, or serve them, or bow down yourselves to them, ⁸but cleave to the Lord your God as you have done to this day. ⁹For the Lord has driven out before you great and strong nations; and as for you, no man has been able to withstand you to this day. ¹⁰One man of you puts to flight a thousand, since it is the Lord your God who fights for you, as he promised you. ¹¹Take good heed to yourselves, therefore, to love the Lord your God. ¹²For if you turn back, and join the remnant of these nations left here among you, and make marriages with them, so that you marry their women and they yours, ¹³know assuredly that the Lord your God will not continue to drive out these nations before you; but they shall be a snare and a trap for you, a scourge on your sides, and thorns in your eyes, till you perish from off this good land which the Lord your God has given you.

Though the word "covenant" is not used in this section, clearly in evidence is the covenant formulary which Israel borrowed from the sphere of international relations as a metaphor for her relationship with the Lord. The covenant formulary can best be understood as a "vassal treaty" in which the vassal (Israel) promises obedience to a beneficent Lord (Yahweh). At least three elements of the covenant formulary can be found here: vv. 3-5 enumerate the Lord's acts on Israel's behalf, which serve as a basis for the covenantal relationship, vv. 6-12 list some of the covenant's stipulations which describe the loyalty which the vassal owes to the Lord and v. 13 contains threats of divine action in the face of disloyalty. The covenant formulary with its emphasis on the conditional nature of the relationship between God and Israel fits well within the Deuteronomic theological perspective of those responsible for the final shape of Joshua.

The covenant metaphor emphasizes the conditional nature of Israel's relationship with God and her possession of the land. These are conditioned on her obedience to the Law. A second such indication is the continued presence of remnants of the indigenous Canaanite population in the land which Israel was to inherit (vv. 4-5, 7, 12). These "unconquered" Canaanites are presented as a potential menace to Israel and thereby they remind her that only obedience to the Law can provide rest and security (v. 1).

THE FUTURE OF ISRAEL
23:14-16

[14]"And now I am about to go the way of all of the earth, and you know in your hearts and souls, all of you, that not one thing has failed of all the good things which the Lord your God promised concerning you; all have come to pass for you, not one of them has failed. [15]But just as all the good things which the Lord your God promised concerning you have been fulfilled for you, so the Lord will bring upon you all the evil things, until he have destroyed you from off this good land which the Lord your God has given you, [16]if you transgress the covenant of the Lord your God, which he commanded you, and go and serve other gods and bow down to them. Then the anger of the Lord will be kindled against you, and you

shall perish quickly from off the good land which he has given to you."

Here is another attempt to have events of Joshua's life parallel those of Moses. Just as Moses addressed all Israel prior to his death so Joshua does the same. There is a conscious effort to portray Joshua as continuing the work of Moses. This is not done solely to legitimate Joshua but to demonstrate that the role Moses played in Israel's life continues in those who call Israel to obedience. The first successor of Moses was Joshua but others followed. The New Testament reflects such a view: "The scribes and the Pharisees sit on Moses' seat; so practice and observe whatever they tell you..." (Matt 23:2-3a). Similarly the Mishnah, a second century A.D. code of Rabbinic observance, supports this understanding: "Moses received Torah from Sinai and delivered it to Joshua, and Joshua to the Elders and the Elders to the Prophets, and the Prophets to the men of the Great Synagogue." (*Pirke Aboth* 1:1). While the Mosaic period was crucial to Israel's life, the function Moses played for Israel is in some sense carried on by all who call Israel to obedience (v. 6).

The allusions to the exile in vv. 13 and 16 make it quite clear that this chapter was written at a time when the threats spoken here had taken place. At the very least, these verses reflect the exile of the Northern tribes in 721 B.C. and the danger that existed for Judah at the beginning of the 6th century B.C. More probably they reflect the disaster of 587 B.C., the fall of Jerusalem, and the very grave threat that this disaster posed to the very existence of Israel. This chapter then can be seen as a desperate cry for obedience in the face of the mortal danger that faced Israel.

Joshua's Address at Shechem
24:1-33

Although the previous chapter presents Joshua's farewell address to all Israel, Josh 24:1-28 contains still another address to the tribes. This text does not proport to be Joshua's final words though the notice of his death and burial in vv. 29-30 intends to leave the readers with the impression that they have just read an account of Joshua's final words. The anomaly of having two "farewell addresses" probably can be explained by the reluctance of the final editors of the book to have the story of Joshua end on a somewhat negative and threatening note (23:15-16). The result of Joshua's address in chapter 24 is much more positive and hopeful since the people do follow Joshua's lead by pledging to serve the Lord (v. 24).

The concern of this chapter is an ancient one. It poses the question: "Who is to be worshipped?" Joshua represents the bearers of the Exodus tradition who invite other groups which did not experience the Exodus but who are recognized as ethnically related to the Exodus-group to join a common cult. But Joshua is quick to point out that commitment to Yahweh is incompatible with the service of any other divinity. The God worshipped by Joshua and his group is unique in the sense that commitment to Yahweh must be exclusive. In other words, a syncretist solution to the problem of uniting the tribes is not an option. Joshua presents an either/or alternative. This unwillingness to compromise on the part of the Exodus-group reflects its recognition that the cult of the indigenous Canaanite divinities supports a hierarchic and oppressive social system which it rejects. Yahweh is a God who takes the side of slaves against their masters. How could the freed slaves turn around and serve their masters' gods? It is precisely this bond of a common cult which unites these disparate though ethnically and socially related tribes. These tribes come to be known as Israel and they worship Yahweh.

Joshua's role in uniting the tribes in a common cult is probably at the basis of his position in the Bible's presentation of the "conquest." As we have seen, the Book of Joshua offers a highly idealized description of how Israel came to acquire her land. The Joshua of those narratives is more than an historical figure. But the Joshua of this chapter —

the mediator of the covenant — reflects an historical memory of a very crucial period in the life of the tribes. The leadership that Joshua provided at this point made it quite simple for later generations to attribute the "conquest" to him. In a real sense, Joshua can be described as the founder of Israelite religion in Canaan. He completed the work of Moses, and the covenant of Shechem fulfilled the promise made to the patriarchs regarding the possession of the land. It is no wonder that Joshua is given credit for the "conquest" and all that it represented in terms of the unity of the Israelite tribes in the service of Yahweh.

From a theological point of view, this chapter is a paradigm of reflection on and reinterpretation of ancient traditions. This reinterpretation takes place on two levels simultaneously. First, Joshua's speech in vv. 14-24 is a Deuteronomistic reinterpretation of an older confessional statement found in vv. 2b-13. The latter speaks of divine mercy while the former underscores the necessity of obedience. Similarly the theological motifs found here speak to the Exiles who find an explanation for the disaster of 587 B.C. (v. 20) and hope for another act of divine mercy on Israel's behalf since she can do nothing for herself (v. 12).

THE PREAMBLE
24:1

> **24** Then Joshua gathered all the tribes of Israel to Shechem, and summoned the elders, the heads, the judges, and the officers of Israel; and they presented themselves before God.

The setting for this scene is Shechem, a city which is associated with the patriarchs (Gen 12:6-7; 33:18-20) and went on to become an important Israelite and later Samaritan center. The small Samaritan population which has survived to the present still inhabits Shechem (modern Nablus). The Bible does not record an Israelite conquest of Shechem and archaeology shows no destruction during the time of the Israelite entrance into Canaan. The Israelite occupation of Shechem and the surrounding region probably was made with the agreement of the local population. While the preamble assumes the Israelite identity of all participants in the following events, this text certainly preserves the memory of the incorporation of Shechem into the Israelite confederation. The population of the Shechem region who never experienced the Exodus now join in the service of Yahweh with those who did have that experience.

YAHWEH'S SPEECH
24:2-13

²And Joshua said to all the people, "Thus says the Lord, the God of Israel, 'Your fathers lived of old beyond the Euphrates, Terah, the father of Abraham and of Nahor; and they served other gods. ³Then I took your father Abraham from beyond the River and led him through all the land of Canaan, and made his offspring many. I gave him Isaac; ⁴and to Isaac I gave Jacob and Esau. And I gave Esau the hill country of Seir to possess, but Jacob and his children went down to Egypt. ⁵And I sent Moses and Aaron, and I plagued Egypt with what I did in the midst of it; and afterwards I brought you out. ⁶Then I brought your fathers out of Egypt, and you came to the sea; and the Egyptians pursued your fathers with chariots and horsemen to the Red Sea. ⁷And when they cried to the Lord, he put darkness between you and the Egyptians, and made the sea come upon them and cover them; and your eyes saw what I did to Egypt; and you lived in the wilderness a long time. ⁸Then I brought you to the land of the Amorites, who lived on the other side of the Jordan; they fought with you, and I gave them into your hand, and you took possession of their land, and I destroyed them before you. ⁹Then Balak the son of Zippor, king of Moab, arose and fought against Israel; and he sent and invited Balaam the son of Beor to curse you, ¹⁰but I would not listen to Balaam; therefore he blessed

you; so I delivered you out of his hand. [11]And you went over the Jordan and came to Jericho, and the men of Jericho fought against you, and also the Amorites, the Perizzites, the Canaanites, the Hittites, the Girgashites, the Hivites, and the Jebusites; and I gave them into your hand. [12]And I sent the hornet before you, which drove them out before you, the two kings of the Amorites; it was not by your sword or by your bow. [13]I gave you a land on which you had not labored, and cities which you had not built, and you dwell therein; you eat the fruit of vineyards and oliveyards which you did not plant.'

The messenger formula of the preamble ("Thus says the Lord...") identifies this section as the explicit words of God addressed to the tribes although the words are actually spoken by Joshua. This text resembles the confessional statements found in Deut 6:21-24 and 26:5-9 even though these latter do not begin with Abraham. The focus of this speech is clearly on the interventions of the Lord in behalf of Israel. The emphasis is on divine activity — not on human accomplishment. The picture painted of Yahweh is that of a merciful Lord who has providentially guided the life of Israel from the beginning with Abraham until the occupation of the land. This land was acquired not by the force of her arms but by the power of God (v. 12b). The Exiles would have found some measure of hope in these words since Judah's power was broken by Babylon. If a restoration were to take place, it would not happen except by another exercise of divine power.

There is no mention of Sinai in this summary of Israel's life with God. Quite clearly covenant and law play no essential role in this description of Israel's relationship with God. The clear emphasis here is on the unmerited blessings which Israel has received from Yahweh. Again this would have been good news to the Exiles who could only hope for another such unmerited act of mercy.

JOSHUA'S SPEECH AND THE PEOPLE'S RESPONSE 24:14-24

[14]Now therefore fear the Lord and serve him in sincerity and in faithfulness; put away the gods which your fathers served beyond the River, and in Egypt, and serve the Lord. [15]And if you be unwilling to serve the Lord, choose this day whom you will serve, whether the gods your fathers served in the region beyond the River, or the gods of the Amorites in whose land you dwell; but as for me and my house, we will serve the Lord."

[16]Then the people answered, "Far be it from us that we should forsake the Lord, to serve other gods; [17]for it is the Lord our God who brought us and our fathers up from the land of Egypt, out of the house of bondage, and who did those great signs in our sight, and preserved us in all the way that we went, and among all the peoples through whom we passed; [18]and the Lord drove out before us all the peoples, the Amorites who lived in the land; therefore we also will serve the Lord, for he is our God."

[19]But Joshua said to the people, "You cannot serve the Lord; for he is a holy God; he is a jealous God; he will not forgive your transgressions or your sins. [20]If you forsake the Lord and serve foreign gods, then he will turn and do you harm, and consume you, after having done you good." [21]And the people said to Joshua, "Nay; but we will serve the Lord." [22]Then Joshua said to the people, "You are witnesses against yourselves that you have chosen the Lord, to serve him." And they said, "We are witnesses." [23]He said, "Then put away the foreign gods which are among you, and incline your heart to the Lord, the God of Israel." [24]And the people said to Joshua, "The Lord our God we will serve, and his voice we will obey."

The effect of Joshua's speech is to modulate what was a clear emphasis on mercy and divine initiative in the Lord's speech, vv. 2b-13. Now the concern moves away from a focus on God's activity on Israel's behalf to Israel's responsibilities in view of God's beneficence. This section is certainly a Deuteronomistic reinterpretation of an ancient confessional statement which is quoted as the Lord's own words in the previous section. The expression "fear the Lord" (v. 14) in the sense of serving God occurs fourteen times in Deuteronomy (*e.g.,* "You shall fear the Lord your God; you shall serve him, and swear by his name." Deut 6:13). The obvious concern of the Deuteronomic tradition in general and this passage in particular is to underscore Israel's covenantal responsibilities and to avoid an overemphasis on God's "mighty acts." It may be quite true that God *gave* Israel the land; it is now Israel's duty to *keep* the land by her undivided service to the Lord.

Joshua's reinterpretation of the divine speech obliterates the element of divine mercy which is so clear in vv. 2b-13 and turns those words into a prophecy of doom (vv. 19-20). The people, however, show they desire to enter into covenant with Yahweh and thereby complete the good work which God began in the Exodus and conquest (vv. 16-18).

THE MAKING OF THE COVENANT
24:25-28

> 25So Joshua made a covenant with the people that day, and made statutes and ordinances for them at Shechem. 26And Joshua wrote these words in the book of the law of God; and he took a great stone, and set it up there under the oak in the sanctuary of the Lord. 27And Joshua said to all the people, "Behold, this stone shall be a witness against us; for it has heard all the words of the Lord which he spoke to us; therefore it shall be a witness against you, lest you deal falsely with your God." 28So Joshua sent the people away, every man to his inheritance.

This section is a curious mixture of the old and the new. Setting up of memorial stones was a common cultic practice in the ancient Near East. In fact, such stones have been unearthed by archaeologists at Shechem and have been dated to 1800-1100 B.C. The Deuteronomic tradition did not tolerate such holdovers from pre-Israelite religious practices and the Book of Deuteronomy strictly forbids the erection of such stones (Deut 16:22). Evidently the tradition of a memorial pillar at Shechem was too strong for the Deuteronomist to ignore; however, this old tradition is partially offset by having Joshua, somewhat anachronistically, record the covenant "in the book of the Law of God" (v. 26).

THREE GRAVES
24:29-33

> [29]After these things Joshua the son of Nun, the servant of the Lord, died, being a hundred and ten years old. [30]And they buried him in his own inheritance at Timnath-serah, which is in the hill country of Ephraim, north of the mountain of Gaash.
>
> [31]And Israel served the Lord all the days of Joshua, and all the days of the elders who outlived Joshua and had known all the work which the Lord did for Israel.
>
> [32]The bones of Joseph which the people of Israel brought up from Egypt were buried at Shechem, in the portion of ground which Jacob bought from the sons of Hamor the father of Shechem for a hundred pieces of money; it became an inheritance of the descendants of Joseph.
>
> [33]And Eleazar the son of Aaron died; and they buried him at Gibeah, the town of Phinehas his son, which had been given him in the hill country of Ephraim.

The accounts of the burial places of Joshua, Joseph and Eleazar conclude the book. At his death, Joshua is given the title "the servant of the Lord" which had been reserved for Moses alone (1:1, 7, 15) and which will later be given to David (2 Sam 3:18). The story of Joshua's leadership of the tribes ends on a positive note with regard to Israel's fidelity to Yahweh during the lifetime of Joshua and his immediate successors.

The note regarding the grave of Joseph is included here probably because of the grave's location in Shechem. The same is true regarding the note on Eleazar's burial place. Though the exact site is not known, it too was likely in the neighborhood of Shechem.

THE BOOK OF JUDGES

THE BOOK OF JUDGES

The Introduction to the Period of the Judges
1:1—2:5

The Book of Judges begins with the admission of an undeniable historical fact: Israel's acquisition of the land was incomplete. The consequence of this failure to attain control over all of Canaan was the continued presence of the indigenous Canaanite population in what was to be the inheritance of the Israelite tribes. At first Israel offered a benign explanation for this: a too quick extermination of the Canaanites would have allowed the land to be overrun by wild beasts (Exod 23:29; Deut 7:22). The Book of Judges provides another practical explanation for the survival of the Canaanites: succeeding generations of Israelites need to be introduced to the art of warfare (Judg 3:1b-2).

The book also preserves explanations which have a decidedly theological flavor. If Israel would have obeyed the Lord's commands, her victories over Canaan would have been complete. Since obedience was not forthcoming, the Canaanites will be a continuing problem for the tribes (2:1-5). The survival of the indigenous population of Canaan then is an act of divine judgment upon an unfaithful Israel (2:20-21). Finally the Canaanites are permitted to survive in order that the Lord may test Israel to determine if the nation will obey the "commandments of the Lord" (2:22; 3:1a, 4).

The Deuteronomist knew the answer to that question: Israel failed the test miserably.

The real question facing the Deuteronomist was this: does this failure mean the end of Israel? The story of the era of the Judges shows that divine punishment was just to be sure, but it was always overcome by divine mercy. Even though Israel did not show herself to be faithful, the Lord's compassion always overcame the Lord's justice. The Exile seemed to be different. It appeared as if the Lord's mercy was exhausted and Israel had to face the full force of the Lord's punishment. The Deuteronomist's telling of the ancient stories about Israel's judges was an act of faith in and hope for still another act of divine mercy.

THE PRE-EMINENCE OF JUDAH
1:1-21

1   After the death of Joshua the people of Israel inquired of the Lord, "Who shall go up first for us against the Canaanites, to fight against them?" ²The Lord said, "Judah shall go up; behold, I have given the land into his hand." ³And Judah said to Simeon his brother, "Come up with me into the territory allotted to me, that we may fight against the Canaanites; and I likewise will go with you into the territory allotted to you." So Simeon went with him. ⁴Then Judah went up and the Lord gave the Canaanites and the Perizzites into their hand; and they defeated ten thousand of them at Bezek. ⁵They came upon Adonibezek at Bezek, and fought against him, and defeated the Canaanites and the Perizzites. ⁶Adonibezek fled; but they pursued him, and caught him, and cut off his thumbs and his great toes. ⁷And Adonibezek said, "Seventy kings with their thumbs and great toes cut off used to pick up scraps under my table; as I have done, so God has requited me." And they brought him to Jerusalem, and he died there.

⁸And the men of Judah fought against Jerusalem, and took it, and smote it with the edge of the sword, and set

the city on fire. [9]And afterward the men of Judah went down to fight against the Canaanites who dwelt in the hill country, in the Negeb, and in the lowland. [10]And Judah went against the Canaanites who dwelt in Hebron (now the name of Hebron was formerly Kiriatharba); and they defeated Sheshai and Ahiman and Talmai.

[11]From there they went against the inhabitants of Debir. The name of Debir was formerly Kiriathsepher. [12]And Caleb said, "He who attacks Kiriathsepher and takes it, I will give him Achsah my daughter as wife." [13]And Othniel the son of Kenaz, Caleb's younger brother, took it; and he gave him Achsah his daughter as wife. [14]When she came to him, she urged him to ask her father for a field; and she alighted from her ass, and Caleb said to her, "What do you wish?" [15]She said to him, "Give me a present; since you have set me in the land of the Negeb, give me also springs of water." And Caleb gave her the upper springs and the lower springs.

[16]And the descendants of the Kenite, Moses' father-in-law, went up with the people of Judah from the city of palms into the wilderness of Judah, which lies in the Negeb near Arad; and they went and settled with the people. [17]And Judah went with Simeon his brother, and they defeated the Canaanites who inhabited Zephath, and utterly destroyed it. So the name of the city was called Hormah. [18]Judah also took Gaza with its territory, and Ashkelon with it territory, and Ekron with its territory. [19]And the Lord was with Judah, and he took possession of the hill country, but he could not drive out the inhabitants of the plain, because they had chariots of iron. [20]And Hebron was given to Caleb, as Moses had said; and he drove out from it the three sons of Anak. [21]But the people of Benjamin did not drive out the Jebusites who dwelt in Jerusalem; so the Jebusites have dwelt with the people of Benjamin in Jerusalem to this day.

The Book of Judges begins with a crisis of leadership. With the death of Joshua the tribes are without a military leader. A number of local traditions has been assembled with the purpose of highlighting the important position occupied by the tribe of Judah. From an historical point of view, this tribe probably did not emerge with its own identity until the time of David under whose leadership it achieved a place of prominence among the Israelite tribes. Here the achievements of the various groups that went into the composition of Judah are listed in annalistic fashion, *i.e.*, without any narrative elaboration. These groups include Simeon (v. 4), Caleb (v. 12), the Kenizzites (v. 13) and the Kenites (v. 16). By the time of the monarchy, these groups had long since been assimilated into the dominant tribe of the South — Judah.

While the thrust of this text is to underscore the role of Judah in the period after Joshua's death, vv. 17-19 clearly indicate that Judah was able to occupy only the hills of southern Canaan. The fertile plains remained under non-Israelite control (v. 19). The reason given for this is the superior armaments of the Canaanites, especially their "chariots of iron." Of course, these chariots were not made of iron but of wood and leather. Iron was probably used only for the joints and fittings or for decorating the chariots. Nonetheless a chariot force could cause havoc to infantry without such equipment. Since chariots can be maneuvered only in large, open areas, it is no wonder that the plains remained under Canaanite control and the hills were the only Israelite enclave. Here the only reason given for Israel's failure to occupy the plains is a military one. The Deuteronomist is content to make use of this ancient tradition from the South to revive the memory that even under Judah's leadership, the conquest was only partially successful.

Two details of this passage call for special comment. First is the mutilation of the kings in v. 7. This may have been an attempt to invalidate their royal status as symbolized through anointing. (Note that the anointing of the priest includes placing blood on Aaron's right ear, thumb and big toe, *cf.,* Exod 29:20). Secondly Jerusalem was not brought into Israel until the time of David, yet v. 8 speaks about

Judah's victory over that city. Josh 15:13 states that Judah *did not* take Jerusalem and Judg 1:21 states that Benjamin failed as well. Perhaps the tribes did enjoy some initial success against Jerusalem, but were not in a position to consolidate their victory.

THE "NONCONQUEST" OF THE NORTH 1:22-36

22The house of Joseph also went up against Bethel; and the Lord was with them. 23And the house of Joseph sent to spy out Bethel. (Now the name of the city was formerly Luz.) 24And the spies saw a man coming out of the city, and they said to him, "Pray, show us the way into the city, and we will deal kindly with you." 25And he showed them the way into the city; and they smote the city with the edge of the sword, but they let the man and all his family go. 26And the man went to the land of the Hittites and built a city, and called its name Luz; that is its name to this day.

27Manasseh did not drive out the inhabitants of Bethshean and its villages, or Taanach and its villages, or the inhabitants of Dor and its villages, or the inhabitants of Ibleam and its villages, or the inhabitants of Megiddo and its villages; but the Canaanites persisted in dwelling in that land. 28When Israel grew strong, they put the Canaanites to forced labor, but did not utterly drive them out.

29And Ephraim did not drive out the Canaanites who dwelt in Gezer; but the Canaanites dwelt in Gezer among them.

30Zebulun did not drive out the inhabitants of Kitron, or the inhabitants of Nahalol; but the Canaanites dwelt among them, and became subject to forced labor.

31Asher did not drive out the inhabitants of Acco, or the inhabitants of Sidon, or of Ahlab, or of Achzib, or of Helbah, or of Aphik, or of Rehob; 32but the Asherites dwelt among the Canaanites, the inhabitants of the land; for they did not drive them out.

33Naphtali did not drive out the inhabitants of Bethshemesh, or the inhabitants of Bethanath, but dwelt among the Canaanites, the inhabitants of the land; nevertheless the inhabitants of Bethshemesh and of Bethanath became subject to forced labor for them.

³⁴The Amorites pressed the Danites back into the hill country, for they did not allow them to come down to the plain; ³⁵the Amorites persisted in dwelling in Harheres, in Aijalon, and in Shaalbim, but the hand of the house of Joseph rested heavily upon them, and they became subject to forced labor. ³⁶And the border of the Amorites ran from the ascent of Akrabbim, from Sela and upward.

Though the Book of Joshua did not describe an Israelite victory over Bethel, archaeology has revealed that the city was destroyed in the early 13th century B.C. It is interesting to note that the only victory recounted here in chap. 1 is one over Bethel which was later to become the site of a temple built by Jeroboam I to rival that of Jerusalem (*cf.*, 1 Kgs 12:25-30). Dan, the site of another of Jeroboam's temples, is the last Canaanite city whose conquest is described (Judg 18:27-31). The Deuteronomistic tradition considered these sanctuaries to be idolatrous. These allusions which frame the Book of Judges must be portents of the evil ahead for Israel (*cf.*, 2 Kgs 17).

Other than Joseph's success against Bethel, the rest of this section lists the failures of the Israelite tribes in the North. While the list is not complete (Reuben, Gad and Issachar are not mentioned), the over-all impression is clear enough: the Israelite tribes were too weak to expel the Canaanites. Again Israel's failures are explained in military rather than theological terms. The sites mentioned in this passage were small city-states which controlled commercial traffic through a web of dependent villages. Because the tribes were not able to overcome the power of these city-states, the Israelites developed a *modus vivendi* with the Canaanites — something outlawed in Judg 2:2a. During the time of David, Israel was powerful enough to finally integrate these city-states into the Israelite Empire.

The phrase "when Israel grew strong" (v. 28) probably

refers to the era of Israelite power under David. The irony of the situation is that a nation that remembered forced labor as part of its own oppressive history made use of the same system when it suited its purposes (vv. 28, 30, 33, 35). The establishement of this "feudal" structure came with the rise of the monarchy which replaced early Israel's egalitarian social system with the hierarchical social system which was characteristic of the Canaanite city-states. It is more correct to say then that these Canaanite city-states were not really integrated into the Israelite social system but that an Israelite overlord simply replaced the Canaanite one.

This passage, however, should not be seen as an indictment of the monarchy; rather, its purpose is to show how Israel foundered after the death of Joshua. Without someone providing the kind of leadership that Moses and Joshua gave to Israel, the tribes could not be successful. The best they could do was to make some sort of living arrangement with the Canaanite city-states and bide their time until the conquest of Canaan could be completed.

DIVINE JUDGMENT
2:1-5

> **2** Now the angel of the Lord went up from Gilgal to Bochim. And he said, "I brought you up from Egypt, and brought you into the land which I swore to give your fathers. I said, 'I will never break my covenant with you, ²and you shall make no covenant with the inhabitants of this land; you shall break down their altars.' But you have not obeyed my command. What is this you have done? ³So now I say, I will not drive them out before you; but they shall become adversaries to you, and their gods shall be a snare to you." ⁴When the angel of the Lord spoke these words to all the people of Israel, the people lifted up their voices and wept. ⁵And they called the name of that place Bochim; and they sacrificed there to the Lord.

Bochim is a place name which occurs nowhere else in the Hebrew Bible. The Greek version of the Old Testament has

Bethel in place of Bochim. Again animosity towards the sanctuary at Bethel prevented an explicit reference to this cultic site since it later was to become a rival of Jerusalem. This text probably originated as an attempt to legitimate the Israelite appropriation of a Canaanite sanctuary which was connected with a ritual of weeping for a "deceased" vegetation deity (*cf.*, Zech 12:11; Ezek 8:14). The theophany which is used to support an Israelite cult at Bochim/Bethel is associated with an angelic apparition both here (vv. 1, 4) and in Gen 28:12 which offers another Israelite cultic tradition connected with the same site.

The Deuteronomist uses this ancient cultic legend as a vehicle to excoriate Israel for its tendency to assimilate with the Canaanites. This process of assimilation involved not only the cultic sphere but especially the socio-political. Canaanite religion provided a theoretical support structure for a hierarchical and oppressive social system. Worshipping Canaanite gods meant not only apostasy from Yahweh but also abandonment of the egalitarian and decentralized social system supported by Yahwism. In the eyes of the Deuteronomist, this easy toleration of non-Israelite religious systems was the downfall of Israel. This fatal tendency began already in the tribal era when the Israelites refused to expel the Canaanites and destroy their altars, preferring instead to make covenants with them (v. 2a). While the text seems to present the conflict between Canaan and Israel as an ethnic and religious one, the conflict spilled over into the social and political realms as well. It could not be otherwise, given the ancient Near Eastern worldview in which the religious and the political formed one reality.

Israel Under the Judges
2:6—3:6

THE DEATH OF JOSHUA
2:6-10

> [6]When Joshua dismissed the people, the people of Israel went each to his inheritance to take possession of

the land. [7]And the people served the Lord all the days of Joshua, and all the days of the elders who outlived Joshua, who had seen all the great work which the Lord had done for Israel. [8]And Joshua the son of Nun, the servant of the Lord, died at the age of one hundred and ten years. [9]And they buried him within the bounds of his inheritance in Timnathheres, in the hill country of Ephraim, north of the mountain of Gaash. [10]And all that generation also were gathered to their fathers; and there arose another generation after them, who did not know the Lord or the work which he had done for Israel.

Before the Deuteronomist begins telling the story of the Judges, the reader is reminded of the basic problem faced by Israel in her early years in the land: the vacuum of leadership. With the death of Joshua and his generation, Israel was bereft of the type of leadership that insured her fidelity to the Lord. This text is basically the same as that found in Josh 24:28-31. Its repetition here underscores the reason for Israel's crisis. The death of Joshua marks the end of an era since the new generation does not "know the Lord" (v. 10b).

ISRAEL'S FAILURE
2:11-15

[11]And the people of Israel did what was evil in the sight of the Lord and served the Baals; [12]and they forsook the Lord, the God of their fathers, who had brought them out of the land of Egypt; they went after other gods, from among the gods of the peoples who were round about them, and bowed down to them; and they provoked the Lord to anger. [13]They forsook the Lord, and served the Baals and the Ashtaroth. [14]So the anger of the Lord was kindled against Israel, and he gave them over to plunderers, who plundered them; and he sold them into the power of their enemies round about, so that they could no longer withstand their enemies. [15]Whenever they

> marched out, the hand of the Lord was against them for
> evil, as the Lord had warned, and as the Lord had sworn
> to them; and they were in sore straits.

If Israel no longer "knows Yahweh," there is only one
possibility for her: idolatry. Here the Baals and Ashtaroth
refer not to specific deities but are symbolic of non-
Yahwistic worship in general. The evil which Israel did in
serving these gods was not simply a religious offense; it had
important socio-political consequences. The strength and
unity of the tribes were cemented by their common service
of Yahweh. Once loyalty to Yahweh became compromised,
the tribes could not function with any cohesiveness. The
tribes became easy prey for those who opposed their novel
social system in which all power and authority were ascribed
to Yahweh, a non-human lord. It was in the interest of the
Canaanite hierarchy to eliminate this new element which was
rending the socio-political fabric then in place. Israel coop-
erated in her own destruction by going over to the Canaanite
side by worshipping the Baals and the Ashtaroth (v. 13).

YAHWEH'S RESPONSE
2:16-23

> [16]Then the Lord raised up judges, who saved them out
> of the power of those who plundered them. [17]And yet they
> did not listen to their judges; for they played the harlot
> after other gods and bowed down to them; they soon
> turned aside from the way in which their fathers had
> walked, who had obeyed the commandments of the Lord,
> and they did not do so. [18]Whenever the Lord raised up
> judges for them, the Lord was with the judge, and he
> saved them from the hand of their enemies all the days of
> the judge; for the Lord was moved to pity by their groan-
> ing because of those who afflicted and oppressed them.
> [19]But whenever the judge died, they turned back and
> behaved worse than their fathers, going after other gods,
> serving them and bowing down to them; they did not

drop any of their practices or their stubborn ways. [20]So the anger of the Lord was kindled against Israel; and he said, "Because this people have transgressed my covenant which I commanded their fathers, and have not obeyed my voice, [21]I will not henceforth drive out before them any of the nations that Joshua left when he died, [22]that by them I may test Israel, whether they will take care to walk in the way of the Lord as their fathers did, or not." [23]So the Lord left those nations, not driving them out at once, and he did not give them into the power of Joshua.

Despite this infidelity, Yahweh does not abandon Israel. Even though the people do not appeal to the Lord in their difficulty, Yahweh raises up "judges" to save Israel from her enemies (v. 16). In v. 17 the judge is portrayed as a prophet who calls Israel to obedience. While this portrait is not in harmony with the manner the judges are portrayed in the rest of the book, it does serve the Deuteronomist's purpose well since he presents the judges as filling the vacuum of leadership caused by the death of Joshua. Unfortunately this crisis of leadership recurred with the same bad effects when each judge died (v. 19). The Deuteronomist describes a pattern of punishment and of mercy (vv. 18-19). Israel's future is dependent not so much on her ability to be faithful to Yahweh as much as it is dependent upon the Lord's mercy. In other words, the Lord does not respond to Israel's assimilation of the Canaanite way of life with complete and absolute rejection of Israel. There is, instead, divine discipline followed by salvation. The question which is obvious is how long can all this go on? Is there no limit to the Lord's mercy?

SUMMARY
3:1-6

3 Now these are the nations which the Lord left, to test Israel by them, that is, all in Israel who had no experience of any war in Canaan; ²it was only that the generations of the people of Israel might know war, that he might teach war to such at least as had not known it before. ³These are the nations: the five lords of the Philistines, and all the Canaanites, and the Sidonians, and the Hivites who dwelt on Mount Lebanon, from Mount Baalhermon as far as the entrance of Hamath. ⁴They were for the testing of Israel, to know whether Israel would obey the commandments of the Lord, which he commanded their fathers by Moses. ⁵So the people of Israel dwelt among the Canaanites, the Hittites, the Amorites, the Perizzites, the Hivites, and the Jebusites; ⁶and they took their daughters to themselves for wives, and their own daughters they gave to their sons; and they served their gods.

Again it is clear that the association with Canaanite culture is not limited to the religious sphere. Intermarriage (v. 6) could only serve to weaken further the bonds of unity that existed between the Israelite tribes. Israel's compromises with the Canaanites will mean continuing problems for her. The Canaanites and their culture will be a lure enticing Israel away from her fidelity to the Lord (v. 4). Verse 5 reproduces a fairly stereotyped list of peoples who will be a source of difficulties for Israel. The stories of the judges which follow show that strong leadership offered by someone committed to Yahweh could extricate Israel from the consequences of her folly.

The Exploits of Israel's Judges
3:7—16:31

OTHNIEL
3:7-11

⁷And the people did what was evil in the sight of the Lord, forgetting the Lord their God, and serving the Baals and the Asheroth. ⁸Therefore the anger of the Lord was kindled against Israel, and he sold them into the hand

of Cushanrishathaim king of Mesopotamia; and the people of Israel served Cushanrishathaim eight years. [9]But when the people of Israel cried to the Lord, the Lord raised up a deliverer for the people of Israel, who delivered them, Othniel the son of Kenaz, Caleb's younger brother. [10]The Spirit of the Lord came upon him, and he judged Israel; he went out to war, and the Lord gave Cushanrishathaim king of Mesopotamia into his hand; and his hand prevailed over Cushanrishathaim. [11]So the land had rest forty years. Then Othniel the son of Kenaz died.

The first story about an individual judge is no story at all. There is no action, no heroic deeds, no narrative but the simple affirmation that Othniel was chosen by the Lord (v. 9), that he judged Israel (v. 10a) and that he led Israel to war and victory (v. 10b).

There are a few problems with the identification of both the protagonist and the antagonist of this piece. First of all Othniel has been associated previously with the settlement period (*cf.*, Josh 15:16-19 and Judg 1:11-15). That he could have been active in both the settlement period and the judges' period is doubtful. Secondly the name of Othniel's opponent is clearly emphasized here since it is mentioned four times while the hero's name is mentioned only twice. Unfortunately the identity of the "twice evil" (Rishtaim) Cushan is otherwise unknown. Similarly the identification of Mesopotamia as Cushan's realm (v. 8) is a problem since Israel did not face any hostility from Mesopotamia during this period. There may be some scribal errors in the transmission of both Cushan's name and realm, but it is hazardous to be any more precise than this.

What is clear from all these difficulties is that the Deuteronomist is more concerned with presenting Othniel as a paradigm of the judge than with providing the readers with precise information about his exploits. In other words, Othniel is the standard of how the post-Joshua leadership is to work. The "Spirit of the Lord" (v. 10) is what makes it possible for Othniel and other judges (*cf.,* 6:34; 11:29) to accomplish extraordinary feats. They become able to commit themselves to ventures that require bravery and resolve.

Three features of this notice about Othniel require specific comment. First Othniel is the only Judge from the territory of Judah yet his achievements are mentioned before all others. Perhaps this is another indication of Judah's preeminence in the eyes of the Deuteronomist (*cf.,* Judg 1:2 and 20:18). Secondly v. 8 ("...and he *sold* them...") portrays Yahweh as a slave trader. This is quite an irony given the basic thrust of Israel's central theological affirmation about God as the Lord who *frees* slaves (*cf.,* Deut 26:6-8). Finally v. 9 introduces the motif of Israel's appeal to Yahweh in the midst of her self-induced troubles. This motif is missing in 2:11-22. There God is moved by Israel's suffering (2:18) — not by any appeals for help. Such appeals can be abused and, in any case, Israel is always dependent upon God's mercy.

EHUD
3:12-30

12And the people of Israel again did what was evil in the sight of the Lord; and the Lord strengthened Eglon the king of Moab against Israel, because they had done what was evil in the sight of the Lord. 13He gathered to himself the Ammonites and the Amalekites, and went and defeated Israel; and they took possession of the city of palms. 14And the people of Israel served Eglon the king of Moab eighteen years.

15But when the people of Israel cried to the Lord, the Lord raised up for them a deliverer, Ehud, the son of Gera, the Benjaminites, a left-handed man. The people of Israel sent tribute by him to Eglon the king of Moab. 16And Ehud made for himself a sword with two edges, a cubit in length; and he girded it on his right thigh under his clothes. 17And he presented the tribute to Eglon king of Moab. Now Eglon was a very fat man. 18And when

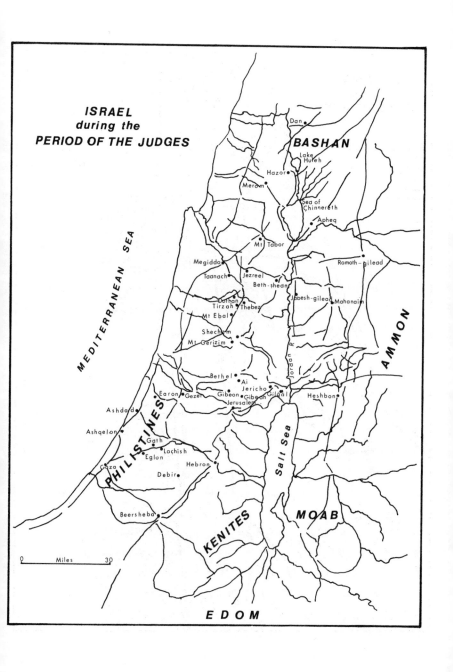

ISRAEL
during the
PERIOD OF THE JUDGES

BASHAN

Dan

Lake
Huleh

Hazor

Merom

Sea of
Chinnereth

Apheq

Mt Tabor

Ramoth – gilead

Megiddo

Taanach

Jezreel

Beth-shean

Jabesh-gilead   Mahanaim

Dothan
Tirzah   Thebez

Mt Ebal

Shechem

Mt Gerizim

AMMON

Bethel

Ai
Jericho

Earon   Gezer   Gibeon   Gibeah   Gilgal   Heshbon
Jerusalem

Ashdad

Ashqelon

Gath

Lachish

Eglon

Gaza

Debir

Hebron

Salt Sea

MOAB

Beersheba

KENITES

0   Miles   30

E D O M

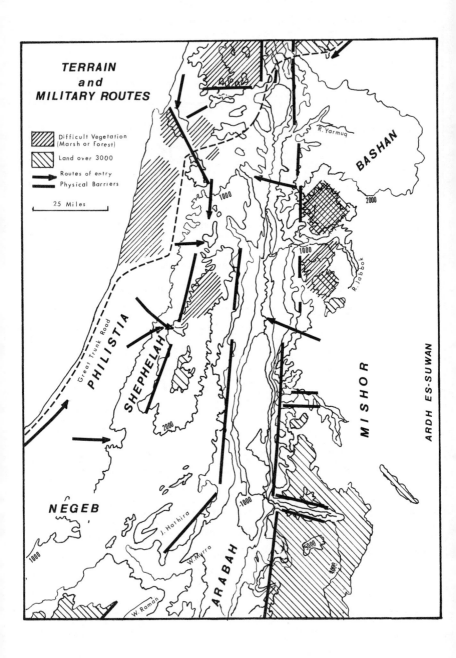

TERRAIN
and
MILITARY ROUTES

Difficult Vegetation
(Marsh or Forest)
Land over 3000
Routes of entry
Physical Barriers

25 Miles

R. Yarmuq

BASHAN

2000

1000

R. Jabbok

1000

Great Trunk Road

PHILISTIA

SHEPHELAH

2000

MISHOR

ARDH ES-SUWAN

NEGEB

J. Hathira

1000

1000

W. Murra

5000

4000

ARABAH

W. Raman

Ehud had finished presenting the tribute, he sent away the people that carried the tribute. ¹⁹But he himself turned back at the sculptured stones near Gilgal, and said, "I have a secret message for you, O king." And he commanded, "Silence," And all his attendants went out from his presence. ²⁰And Ehud came to him, as he was sitting alone in his cool roof chamber. And Ehud said, "I have a message from God for you." And he arose from his seat. ²¹And Ehud reached with his left hand, took the sword from his right thigh, and thrust it into his belly; ²²and the hilt also went in after the blade, and the fat closed over the blade, for he did not draw the sword out of his belly; and the dirt came out. ²³Then Ehud went out into the vestibule, and closed the doors of the roof chamber upon him, and locked them.

²⁴When he had gone, the servants came; and when they saw that the doors of the roof chamber were locked, they thought, "He is only relieving himself in the closet of the cool chamber." ²⁵And they waited till they were utterly at a loss; but when he still did not open the doors of the roof chamber, they took the key and opened them; and there lay their lord dead on the floor.

²⁶Ehud escaped while they delayed, and passed beyond the sculptured stones, and escaped to Seirah. ²⁷When he arrived, he sounded the trumpet in the hill country of Ephraim; and the people of Israel went down with him from the hill country, having him at their head. ²⁸And he said to them, "Follow after me; for the Lord has given your enemies the Moabites into your hand." So they went down after him, and seized the fords of the Jordan against the Moabites, and allowed not a man to pass over. ²⁹And they killed at that time about ten thousand of the Moabites, all strong, able-bodied men; not a man escaped. ³⁰So Moab was subdued that day under the hand of Israel. And the land had rest for eighty years.

The Israelite tribes which were in the process of consolidating their hold on the area west of the Jordan had to deal

with external pressures applied by the Transjordan kingdoms of Moab and Ammon which came on the scene during
the latter part of the 13th century B.C. The story of Ehud is
composed of an ancient heroic saga from the tribe of Benjamin which recalled those early days of struggle together
with a later Deuteronomistic editorial framework which
integrates the Benjaminite tradition into the wider setting of
"all Israel."

Close attention to the geographical details supplied in this
narrative makes it clear that there is some confusion about
the site of Eglon's residence and the path of Ehud's escape.
Resolution of these difficulties is not crucial to understanding the point of either the ancient saga or the Deuteronomistic additions. One geographical note that needs some
comment is the identity of "the city of palms" (v. 13). Both
Deut 34:3 and 2 Chron 28:15 identify Jericho as the city of
palms. The narrative in Judges does not make this identification out of respect for the Deuteronomistic tradition
which held that Jericho was not rebuilt until the monarchic
period (*cf.,* Josh 6:26 and 1 Kgs 16:34). Archaeology,
moreover, supports this latter tradition since excavation has
shown that Jericho was not the site of a major occupation
during the Israelite period until the 7th century B.C. — even
though there was always some habitation in the area. "The
city of palms" does not refer to Jericho but to some sort of
encampment in the vicinity.

Eglon probably used this oasis as the base of his operations west of the Jordan. Though the narrative describes
Eglon as "king of Moab," he was probably no more than a
bandit chieftain from east of the Jordan who made occasional forays into Israelite territory for the purpose of exact-
ing tribute from the defenceless settlers there.

The ancient saga which serves as the basis of this narrative
describes how Ehud, a Benjaminite hero, was able to defeat
Eglon and his band of plunderers. The story contrasts the
cleverness of the Israelites with the stupidity of the Moabites. Ehud is able to smuggle a weapon into Eglon's own
residence (v. 16), to use Eglon's respect for oracles to isolate

the Moabite from his guards (v. 20) and then to make good his escape after the assassination while Eglon's guards stand outside their master's door without any awareness of his plight (vv. 24-26). The Moabites are portrayed as gullible fools. The ease with which Ehud completes his task and makes good his escape is presented as a monument to Moabite ineptness. The story's vivid description of how Ehud's sword is lost amid the paunch of the overweight Eglon and its scatological theme (v. 24) indicate that originally it had no theological purpose. The story was simply a coarse Benjaminite saga about victory over Moabite bandits.

Ehud was able to secure this victory because of the confusion he created among the Moabites by means of his assassination of Eglon. In the ancient world, the death of an army's commander usually involved the dissolution of his forces. The armies of antiquity did not operate with a smooth chain of command which would secure orderly succession. This is especially true of plundering bands like that of Eglon. Ehud's dispatch of Eglon was tantamount to victory over his entire force and the relief of the Israelites who had been paying tribute to Eglon and his plunderers.

The Deuteronomist takes this local Benjaminite sage about the assassination of a Moabite bandit leader and transforms it into the story of a great victory of all Israel over the king of Moab (vv. 27, 30). The vehicle for this transformation is the Deuteronomic theme of Holy War. Note the formulaic expression of v. 28 which reflects the ideology of Holy War. Israel did not have to even fight against Moab. All Israel's troops had to do was station themselves at the fords of the Jordan in order to cut down the retreating Moabites. The number in v. 29 is an exaggeration; all it implies is that Israel enjoyed a great victory. In the ancient world, reports of military victories were often couched in stereotyped language which usually did not reflect the actual results of armed conflicts.

The ancient saga (vv. 15b-25) portrays Ehud as the representative who was of the Benjaminites chosen to bring their tribute to Eglon. He is not designated by the Lord nor endowed with the spirit. Even "the word of God" (v. 20) is a ruse which Ehud uses in his plot. On the other hand, the Deuteronomistic redaction (vv. 12-15a; 26-30) transforms Ehud into a deliverer raised up by the Lord to lead all Israel to a great victory. The effect of the redaction is to change a local Benjaminite tradition about the assassination of a bandit leader into an all-Israelite saga of victory in Holy War against the king of Moab.

SHAMGAR
3:31

> [31] After him was Shamgar the son of Anath, who killed six hundred of the Philistines with an oxgoad; and he too delivered Israel.

Since 4:1 concludes the story of Ehud by mentioning his death, this one-verse note about Shamgar is clearly an addition to the story of Israel's judges. It is placed here because Shamgar is named in 5:6 as living before the time of Deborah.

This very brief note contains none of the elements that are found in other stories about the judges. There is no mention of a divine call nor of any tribal association. The length of Shamgar's rule and his place of burial go unmentioned. The Deuteronomists had very little information about this judge. What they did know is that Shamgar was an opponent of the Philistines, who were among pre-monarchic Israel's most troubling enemies. Not only did Shamgar oppose the Philistines, but he also inflicted a grave defeat upon them with the most inadequate of weapons. The name Shamgar ben Anath indicates that the hero was not a worshipper of Yahweh but of the goddess Anath. In spite of this, his victory over the Philistines allows him to be included among the judges with the comment that he "*too* delivered Israel."

DEBORAH AND BARAK
4:1—5:31

The achievements of Deborah and Barak are presented by two texts with very different forms. The first follows a familiar pattern: a prose narrative about an Israelite victory (4:4-22) framed by a Deuteronomistic introduction and conclusion (4:1-3; 23-24). The second text (chap 5) is a heroic poem, which is considered the most ancient Israelite literary piece which has survived. The chronological tag line at the end of this chapter (5:31b) which properly belongs at the end of chapter 4 indicates that the editors did wish to unite these two very different texts.

While the agreement between these two accounts of Israelite victory under Deborah and Barak is substantial, there are some differences. A few of these go beyond the simple differences between a prosaic and poetic account of the same event. For example, in the poem the enemy of Israel is Sisera who appears to be acting on his own initiative. According to the prose account, Sisera is acting on behalf of his king, Jabin of Canaan.

This leads to a second problem: the relationship between Judg 4-5 and Josh 11. According to Josh 11:1-11, Jabin, king of Hazor, was defeated by the Israelite tribes and his city was razed. Archaeology does confirm that Hazor was indeed destroyed in the 13th century. Who then is the Jabin of Judg 4-5? First of all, it is clear that Josh 11 and Judg 4-5 are not simply two versions of the same battle. The latter account describes a battle for the control of the fertile Plain of Esdraelon which separates Galilee from central Palestine. The battle described in Josh 11 took place farther north in Upper Galilee and was occasioned by the conflict between the newly settled Israelite tribes and the local Canaanite population. While Jabin's name may be properly associated with the victory of Israel over Hazor (Josh 11), it is clearly a secondary addition in Judg 4. Note that Jabin's name is found in the Deuteronomistic framework to chapter 4 (vv. 2, 23-24; v. 7 is probably a Deuteronomistic addition as

well) and not at all in the poetic account of Chapter 5.
Usually prose narratives are more liable to such secondary
additions than poetic texts which become relatively fixed
and stable. Finally in Judg 4:2 Jabin is given an historically
inaccurate title ("king of Canaan") while in Josh 11:1 he
bears the more plausible title, "king of Hazor."

Credit for the victories at Merom (Josh 11) and Kishon
(Judg 4-5) was given in tradition to the tribes of Zebulon
and Naphtali in whose territories these battles took place.
This influenced, in a rather confused way, the descriptions
of both battles. One element all three accounts have in
common is the Holy War ideology behind them all: it is the
Lord who gives Israel victory over her enemies (Josh 11:6,
Judg 4:7; 5:11).

The Deuteronomistic Introduction
4:1-3

> **4** And the people of Israel again did what was evil in the
> sight of the Lord, after Ehud died. ²And the Lord sold
> them into the hand of Jabin king of Canaan, who reigned
> in Hazor; the commander of his army was Sisera, who
> dwelt in Haroshethhagoiim. ³Then the people of Israel
> cried to the Lord for help; for he had nine hundred
> chariots of iron, and oppressed the people of Israel
> cruelly for twenty years.

The story of Deborah begins with the usual notes typical
of such Deuteronomistic introductions in Judges: the apostasy of Israel after the death of the previous judge (v. 1), the
"selling" of Israel into the hands of her enemies (v. 2a),
Israel's cry for help (v. 3a) and the length of Israel's subjection (v. 3c). In addition to this expected information, two
personal names are given. The first is Sisera, who surfaces
throughout this chapter and in the next as Israel's antagonist. Sisera serves as the commander of Jabin's army (v. 2).
The latter is given the title "king of Canaan," a title which
never existed since Canaan was not a political entity.
Canaan was composed of a number of city-states. The name

Sisera is not Semitic. Israel's antagonist here may have been a Philistine even though the Philistines are not mentioned in the descriptions of the battle. In fact, Israel's enemies here are not mentioned though they must have been the city-states of the Esdraelon Plain which is the scene of the battle and which Israel previously had not captured (*cf.*, Judg 1:27).

The number of chariots (v. 3b) seems to be extremely high. If it is accurate, such a force would not have been mustered to fight the Israelites but a more formidable enemy such as Egypt. In all likelihood, however, the number is a Deuteronomistic flourish to emphasize the hopeless situation in which Israel found herself as a result of her disobedience.

Deborah Incites Barak
4:4-10

⁴Now Deborah, a prophetess, the wife of Lappidoth, was judging Israel at that time. ⁵She used to sit under the palm of Deborah between Ramah and Bethel in the hill country of Ephraim; and the people of Israel came up to her for judgment. ⁶She sent and summoned Barak the son of Abinoam from Kedesh in Naphtali, and said to him, "The Lord, the God of Israel, commands you, "Go, gather your men at Mount Tabor, taking ten thousand from the tribe of Naphtali and the tribe of Zebulun. ⁷And I will draw out Sisera, the general of Jabin's army, to meet you by the river Kishon with his chariots and his troops; and I will give him into your hand.' " ⁸Barak said to her, "If you will go with me, I will go; but if you will not go with me, I will not go." ⁹And she said, "I will surely go with you; nevertheless, the road on which you are going will not lead to your glory, for the Lord will sell Sisera into the hand of a woman." Then Deborah arose, and went with Barak to Kedesh. ¹⁰And Barak summoned Zebulun and Naphtali to Kedesh; and ten thousand men went up at his heels; and Deborah went up with him.

The account of Israel's victory over Sisera properly begins with the introduction of the two Israelite protagonists. The first and more important is Deborah. Surprisingly the principal leader on the Israelite side is a woman. In fact, the story is dominated by women as we will see. Deborah is called a "prophetess." While ancient Near Eastern sources describe a number of female prophets with political involvements, Deborah is the only such woman in the Old Testament though both Miriam (Exod 15:20) and Huldah (2 Kgs 22:14) are called prophetesses. The latter two do not appear to have any political influence. Though Deborah's husband is named (v. 4), he has no role to play in the story and no other details are given about him. Another unique feature of this narrative is that Deborah is described as a judge who functioned in the juridical, forensic sense (vv. 4-5) before she became a judge in the religious, political sense. Deborah made the transition when she enlisted Barak to raise an army to fight Sisera. Acting as an agent of divine/human communication, the prophetess informed Barak of his divine designation as Israel's field commander and she pronounced an oracle which assured him of victory (v. 7).

Barak's response to Deborah's oracle was less than enthusiastic. He was unwilling to risk any military moves without the assurance of Deborah's presence with the army. He did not wish to be in a position to take sole responsibility in case of failure. Deborah provided the necessary guarantees but added that he would not be able to claim any credit for the eventual victory since it will be God's victory which is to be consolidated by a woman!

The portrait of Deborah's activity as a prophet reflects a tendency discernible in the Deuteronomistic History to portray the prophets in a favorable light and more importantly, to show that obedience to the prophet is always beneficial. Barak obeys and victory results. If only Israel would have obeyed the prophets sent to her, then her situation would be decidedly different from what it became (1 Kgs 17:13-14).

The final preliminary detail is the mustering of the troops at Kedesh (v. 10) in Upper Galilee. The site is just a few miles north of Hazor and its location may be the reason for the introduction of Jabin into the story. While the number of troops mentioned in v. 10 is probably an exaggeration, the muster of Naphtali and Zebulon is understandable since these two tribes would have been involved in any struggle for control of the Plain of Esdraelon.

The Kenites
4:11

> ¹¹Now Heber the Kenite had separated from the Kenites, the descendants of Hobab the father-in-law of Moses, and had pitched his tent as far away as the oak in Zaanannim, which is near Kedesh.

At this point a parenthetic note interrupts the narrative. While it may seem intrusive here, the note is crucial for the conclusion of the story. According to Judg 1:16 the Kenites normally live in the Negev, the desert to the south of Judah. The presence of a Kenite family in Upper Galilee means that the family in question has separated itself from the larger group. The Kenites are described as related to the Israelites through the marriage of Moses to the daughter of Hobab. Other traditions remember Moses' father-in-law as a Midianite named Jethro (Exod 3:1) or Reuel (Exod 2:18). Another tradition names Hobab as the son of Reuel (Num 10:29). While the name of Moses' father-in-law may not be certain, it is clear that the Kenites, a Midianite clan, claimed a relationship with Israel through Moses' father-in-law, who was remembered as one of their number.

The Battle
4:12-16

> ¹²When Sisera was told that Barak the son of Abinoam had gone up to Mount Tabor, ¹³Sisera called out all his chariots, nine hundred chariots of iron, and all the men who were with him, from Haroshethhagoiim to the river Kishon. ¹⁴And Deborah said to Barak, "Up! For this is the day in which the Lord has given Sisera into your

hand. Does not the Lord go out before you?" So Barak went down from Mount Tabor with ten thousand men following him. ¹⁵And the Lord routed Sisera and all his chariots and all his army before Barak at the edge of the sword; and Sisera alighted from his chariot and fled away on foot. ¹⁶And Barak pursued the chariots and the army to Haroshethhagoiim, and all the army of Sisera fell by the edge of the sword; not a man was left.

The battle against the forces led by Sisera is described in language typical of the Holy War ideology: a far superior force is defeated without the use of arms. "The Lord routed Sisera" (v. 15); all Israel had to do was to consolidate the victory by destroying Sisera's retreating army. The narrative's silence with regard to the contributions made by Deborah and Barak or even by the Israelite army underscores the affirmation of faith which ascribes Israel's military victories to God alone.

The upshot of this battle for control of the Esdraelon Plain was that this most important area passed from Canaanite hegemony to that of the Israelite tribes. The tribes of the Northern and Central regions were now in a position to strengthen the bonds of unity that existed between them. Unfortunately the battles for this region were not over. The Israelites eventually had to face the Philistines who recognized the importance of the Esdraelon Plain in their own plans for controlling Palestine (*cf.,* 1 Sam 4).

Sisera's Death
4:17-22

¹⁷But Sisera fled away on foot to the tent of Jael, the wife of Heber the Kenite; for there was peace between Jabin the king of Hazor and the house of Heber the Kenite. ¹⁸And Jael came out to meet Sisera, and said to him, "Turn aside, my lord, turn aside to me; have no fear." So he turned aside to her into the tent, and she covered him with a rug. ¹⁹And he said to her, "Pray, give me a little water to drink; for I am thirsty." So she opened

a skin of milk and gave him a drink and covered him. [20]And he said to her, "Stand at the door of the tent, and if any man comes and asks you, 'Is any one here?' say, No." [21]But Jael the wife of Heber took a tent peg, and took a hammer in her hand, and went softly to him and drove the peg into his temple, till it went down into the ground, as he was lying fast asleep from weariness. So he died. [22]And behold, as Barak pursued Sisera, Jael went out to meet him, and said to him, "Come, and I will show you the man whom you are seeking." So he went in to her tent; and there lay Sisera dead, with the tent peg in his temple.

In contrast to the stereotypical language of the previous section, the narrative continues by describing Sisera's death in a very vivid and colorful manner. After his defeat, Sisera does not flee directly to his own base of operations (Harosheth, v. 2) but he seeks refuge among the Kenites with whom he felt secure. The text indicates that "peace" existed between the Kenites and the Canaanites of Upper Galilee (v. 17). This peace implied not only an absence of hostilities but the existence of a positive relationship based on loyalty, cooperation and covenant. Apparently Jael also felt an obligation of loyalty to the Israelites. Perhaps the Kenites wished to maintain good relationships with both groups who were locked in conflict for the domination of the land. When the conflict reached her door step, Jael had to choose between the Israelites and the Canaanites. The scene is not a pretty one, but it is a dramatic reminder of all that was involved in Israel's acquisition of her land.

This episode blunts the force of the previous section in which Israel's victory is really the Lord's victory. Here the victory is achieved through a treacherous act of assassination. While this does not fit well within the Deuteronomistic perspective, the memory of Jael and her act (*cf.,* 5:24-27) remained etched in Israel's collective memory to the extent that it could not be ignored. In later years, Israel found herself being pulled in different directions by conflicting loyalties. Unlike Jael Israel often made the wrong choices.

Perhaps the Deuteronomist included this piece about Jael as an incitement to loyalty on Israel's part. Israel must choose Yahweh above all others no matter what consequences this choice may entail.

The Deuteronomistic Conclusion
4:23-24

> [23]So on that day God subdued Jabin the king of Canaan before the people of Israel. [24]And the hand of the people of Israel bore harder and harder on Jabin the king of Canaan, until they destroyed Jabin king of Canaan.

One element of the conclusion, *i.e.*, the chronological note about the length of the land's peace under the judge, is interrupted by the Song of Deborah (5:1-31a). It does appear in 5:31b. As has been noted, the mention of Jabin here is anachronistic and the title "king of Canaan" has no precedent in biblical literature or in other ancient Near Eastern documents.

The Song of Deborah
5:1

> 5   Then sang Deborah and Barak the son of Abinoam on that day:

This verse introduces a poetic reflection on the same events described in narrative form in the previous chapter: the rout of a Canaanite army and the death of its general. Though the poem describes the victory won by those who fight in the name of Israel's God, still the final and telling blow against Israel's enemies is delivered by a non-Israelite woman. Deliverance can come from the most unexpected quarters. Though the Song of Deborah is among the most ancient Biblical texts (composed not long after the events celebrated in it), its message spoke to Israel's situation at every moment of her life — especially during her Exile.

The Preliminaries
5:2-8

> 2"That the leaders took the lead in Israel,
>   that the people offered themselves willingly,
>   bless the LORD!

> 3"Hear, O kings; give ear, O princes;
>   to the LORD I will sing,
>   I will make melody to the LORD, the God of Israel.

> 4"Lord, when thou didst go forth from Seir,
>   when thou didst march from the region of Edom,
>   the earth trembled,
>   and the heavens dropped,
>   yea, the clouds dropped water.
> 5The mountains quaked before the Lord,
>   yon Sinai before the LORD, the God of Israel.

> 6"In the days of Shamgar, son of Anath,
>   in the days of Jael, caravans ceased
>   and travelers kept to the byways.
> 7The peasantry ceased in Israel, they ceased
>   until you arose, Deborah,
>   arose as a mother in Israel.
> 8When new gods were chosen,
>   then war was in the gates.
>   Was shield or spear to be seen
>   among forty thousand in Israel?

The poem begins with a call to worship (v. 2-3) which is followed by a description of Yahweh's activity in nature (vv. 4-5) and in Israel's life (vv. 6-8). These three elements make up the first stanza of the poem. This stanza like the others to follow is marked off by an inclusion, *i.e.*, the repetition of an opening word or phrase at the end of a text. In this case the inclusionary phrase is "in Israel" (vv. 2, 8).

After the call to worship, the emphasis in the first stanza falls upon the activity of God, obvious in the cosmic events usually associated with a theophany, *i.e.,* earthquakes, thunder and storm clouds (vv. 4-5). Later in the poem cosmic elements will participate in the victory over Sisera (vv. 20-21). The theophany of the Lord as the Divine Warrior is also part of Ps 68:8-9. The language and motifs are so similar that one must conclude that the Psalmist used Judg 5:4-5 in composing Ps 68.

Unlike the Psalmist who focuses complete attention on divine activity, the author of the Song moves to praise the human agent of the Lord's victory over Sisera. Deborah appears at a time when Canaanite forces were choking off Israel by endangering effective communication between the tribes. The effect of this threat on Israel's life was the loss of her commitment to the Lord. Israel was looking for security by choosing "new gods" (v. 8) for protection. Once again the Lord steps in to forestall complete apostasy. The reader must conclude that it can be no other than the Lord who is active since it is a woman who leads the army without shield or spear (vv. 7-8). There can be no other explanation for the victory which will follow except that it is the Lord's doing though Deborah is the human agent whom the Lord employs.

Deborah's Call
5:9-13

> [9] My heart goes out to the commanders of Israel
> who offered themselves willingly among the people.
> Bless the Lord.
>
> [10] "Tell of it, you who ride on tawny asses,
> you who sit on rich carpets
> and you who walk by the way.
> [11] To the sound of musicians at the watering places,
> there they repeat the triumphs of the Lord,
> the triumphs of Israel.
>
> "Then down to the gates marched the
> people of the Lord.

12"Awake, awake, Deborah!
    Awake, awake, utter a song!
    Arise, Barak, lead away your captives,
    O son of Abinoam.
13Then down marched the remnant of the noble;
    the people of the Lord marched
        down for him against the mighty.

The second stanza is set off by an inclusion with the word "people" (vv. 9, 13). It focuses on Deborah's efforts to forge a new Israelite coalition in order to seize control of the Esdraelon Plain from the Canaanites who are in a position to limit Israel's effective occupation of the promised land. Deborah became a heroic figure in Israel because she was able to defeat the Canaanites at precisely the place where they were the strongest. The plain was an area where the Canaanites could make good use of their awesome chariot forces. Deborah raises the Israelite troops for battle by singing songs which celebrated the Lord's past victories (v. 12). The final verse celebrates Deborah's success at recruiting the troops which will win the final victory.

The Tribes Respond
5:14-18

14From Ephraim they set out thither
        into the valley,
    following you, Benjamin, with your
        kinsmen;
    from Machir marched down the commanders,
        and from Zebulun those who bear
        the marshal's staff;
15the princes of Issachar came with
        Deborah
    and Issachar faithful to Barak;
        into the valley they rushed forth at
        his heels.
    Among the clans of Reuben
        there were great searchings of heart.

> 16Why did you tarry among the sheepfolds,
>   to hear the piping for the flocks?
> Among the clans of Reuben
>   there were great searchings of heart.
>
> 17Gilead stayed beyond the Jordan;
>   and Dan, why did he abide with the ships?
> Asher sat still at the coast of the sea,
>   settling down by his landings.
> 18Zebulun is a people that jeoparded
>   their lives to the death;
>   Naphtali too, on the heights of the field.

For this description of the tribal muster, the author uses a traditional form: the catalogue of tribes (*cf.,* Gen 49; Deut 33). The texts which list the tribes show considerable variation in form which indicates that this form was frequently adapted and expanded. Here the poet wishes to show the success of Deborah's call to arms so there is a list of tribes gathered for battle even though 4:10 indicates that the campaign against Sisera was waged by only Zebulun and Naphtali. The absence of the southern tribe of Judah from this list reflects the memory of Judah's isolation from the struggles of the other tribes during this period. It is little wonder that the dominant position achieved by Judah through the Davidic dynasty during the monarchic period became a source of irritation for the other tribes. Certainly the ease with which the tribes abandoned the dynasty after the death of Solomon (1 Kgs 13) indicates that no really strong ties were made between Judah and the tribes of central and northern Palestine.

The Battle
5:19-23

> 19"The kings came, they fought;
>   then fought the kings of Canaan,
> at Taanach, by the waters of Megiddo;
>   they got no spoils of silver.
> 20From heaven fought the stars,

> from their courses they fought
>> against Sisera.
> 21The torrent Kishon swept them away,
>> the onrushing torrent, the torrent
>> Kishon.
> March on, my soul, with might!
> 22"Then loud beat the horses' hoofs
>> with the galloping, galloping of his steeds.
>
> 23"Curse Meroz, says the angel of the Lord,
>> curse bitterly its inhabitants,
> because they came not to the help of the Lord,
>> to the help of the Lord against the mighty.

The inclusion which sets off this stanza is the word "come" (vv. 19, 23). The theme of the first stanza is repeated here. The Lord's presence is clear in the powerful forces of the cosmos. One of these forces even became an ally in the battle: the stars fight against Sisera (v. 20). In spite of ascribing the victory to the Lord, human instrumentality is decisive as well. That is why the town of Meroz is censured for its failure to muster along with the rest of the tribal levies (v. 23). The poet does not elaborate on the battle. An epic style is avoided in favor of the simple image of horses in flight (v. 22) — an appropriate symbol of defeat for Sisera's chariotry.

The Battle's Sequel
5:24-31

> 24"Most blessed of women be Jael,
>> the wife of Heber the Kenite,
>> of tent-dwelling women most blessed.
> 25He asked water and she gave him milk,
>> she brought him curds in a lordly bowl.
> 26She put her hand to the tent peg
>> and her right hand to the workman's mallet;
> she struck Sisera a blow,
>> she crushed his head,
>> she shattered and pierced his temple.

27He sank, he fell,
   he lay still at her feet;
  at her feet he sank, he fell;
   where he sank, there he fell dead.

28"Out of the window she peered,
   the mother of Sisera gazed through the lattice:
  'Why is his chariot so long in coming?
   Why tarry the hoofbeats of his chariots?'
29Her wisest ladies make answer,
   nay, she gives answer to herself,
30'Are they not finding and dividing the spoil?—
   A maiden or two for every man;
  spoil of dyed stuffs for Sisera,
   spoil of dyed stuffs embroidered
    for my neck as spoil?'

31"So perish all thine enemies, O Lord!
   But thy friends be like the sun as he
    rises in his might."

While the poet does not linger over the battle, two subsequent scenes attract his attention. The first concerns the deed of Jael. After all of Israel's efforts at breaking the control of the Canaanites over Esdraelon, the final and decisive blow is given by a non-Israelite woman. Thus without undercutting the importance of the tribal armies led by Deborah and Barak, the poet is able to affirm that Israel did not save herself. The land remains as it always was — a pure gift of Yahweh. Here this gift is given in part by blows from the hand of a Kenite woman.

The final scene is a poignant description of the flood of conflicting emotions felt by the women who awaited the return of the Canaanite forces from their encounter with the Israelite tribes. The only way Sisera's mother and the wives of his officers can ease their anxiety is by hoping that their man are spending time with the women of a defeated enemy and by believing that their men were busy amassing booty as gifts (v. 30). The delay of the Canaanite warriors forces their women to look for any excuse to avoid facing a discomforting possibility.

The story of Deborah and Barak is dominated from beginning to end by women. Deborah initiates the Israelite movement against the Canaanites; Jael consolidates the victory. The victory is an important one in the development of an Israelite identity through the unification of the tribes. As long as the Israelite tribes remained confined to the hills of Palestine while the passes and plains were in Canaanite hands, the tribes could never be more than a loose, sectionally defined entity without any cohesion. This move by Deborah to seize control of the Esdraelon Plain is a highly significant step in the development of intertribal unity. It is with good reason then that Deborah is called "mother of Israel" (5:7).

THE STORY OF GIDEON
6:1—8:35

The saga of Gideon covers three chapters in the Book of Judges and is told in three parts: 1) Gideon's vocation (6:1-40); 2) Gideon's battles west of the Jordan (7:1—8:3) and 3) Gideon's battles east of the Jordan (8:4-21). There is a brief epilogue in 8:22-35.

The vocation of Gideon
6:1-40

The Midianite scourge
6:1-10

And the land had rest for forty years.

6   The people of Israel did what was evil in the sight of the Lord; and the Lord gave them into the hand of Midian seven years. ²And the hand of Midian prevailed over Israel; and because of Midian the people of Israel made for themselves the dens which are in the mountains, and the caves and the strongholds. ³For whenever the

Israelites put in seed the Midianites and the Amalekites and the people of the East would come up and attack them; [4]they would encamp against them and destroy the produce of the land, as far as the neighborhood of Gaza, and leave no sustenance in Israel, and no sheep or ox or ass. [5]For they would come up with their cattle and their tents, coming like locusts for number; both they and their camels could not be counted; so that they wasted the land as they came in. [6]And Israel was brought very low because of Midian; and the people of Israel cried for help to the Lord. 7 When the people of Israel cried to the Lord on account of the Midianites, [8]the Lord sent a prophet to the people of Israel; and he said to them, "Thus says the Lord, the God of Israel: I led you up from Egypt, and brought you out of the house of bondage; [9]and I delivered you from the hand of the Egyptians, and from the hand of all who oppressed you, and drove them out before you, and gave you their land; [10]and I said to you, 'I am the Lord your God; you shall not pay reverence to the gods of the Amorites, in whose land you dwell.' But you have not given heed to my voice."

The story of Gideon begins with the familiar Deuteronomistic assumption that Israel's sin is the cause of every catastrophe that she has ever experienced. This Deuteronomistic article of faith is certainly the product of theological reflection upon the meaning of the Exile which came to be understood as the judgment *par excellence* upon the infidelity of Israel. In line with this perspective the Exile should not have caught Israel by surprise for from the very beginning of her life in the land, Yahweh has punished Israel by using other nations. Their invasion of the land and oppression of the people were the products of Israel's sin.

The narrative in question presents the scourge of the Midianites and other plunderers as touching all Israel (vv. 2-6). The problem was not simply the theft of harvested crops, but the destruction of the land itself (v. 5b). If the invaders were not checked, Israel's very existence in the land would come to an end. The Israelite tribes had not yet made their control over the land so secure that it could not be threatened by other groups who were making their own claim on the land and its fruits.

One novel feature of this introduction to the Gideon story is the prophetic indictment of vv. 7-10. The unnamed prophet who speaks to Israel employs the messenger formula ("Thus says the Lord..." v. 8) so characteristic of later prophetic speech. Similarly the use of the Exodus motif as the basis of the indictment is reminiscent of Israel's classical prophets. This section which is clearly intrusive here was added to the Gideon story by those who saw Israel's prophets as providing her with the opportunity for a future in the land. Ignoring the prophet is to court disaster; obeying the prophetic word brings divine blessing. Quite likely the Deuteronomistic Historical Work did go through an edition which attempted to highlight the role of the prophet and the effects of the prophetic word upon Israel. These verses are one product of that edition.

Gideon's call
6:11-24

[11]Now the angel of the Lord came and sat under the oak at Ophrah, which belonged to Joash the Abiezrite, as his son Gideon was beating out wheat in the wine press, to hide it from the Midianites. [12]And the angel of the Lord appeared to him and said to him, "The Lord is with you, you mighty man of valor." [13]And Gideon said to him, "Pray, sir, if the Lord is with us, why then has all this befallen us? And where are all his wonderful deeds which our fathers recounted to us, saying, 'Did not the Lord bring us up from Egypt?' But now the Lord has cast us off, and given us into the hand of Midian." [14]And the Lord turned to him and said, "Go in this might of yours and deliver Israel from the hand of Midian; do not I send you?" [15]And he said to him, "Pray, Lord, how can I deliver Israel? Behold, my clan is the weakest in Manasseh, and I am the least in my family." [16]And the Lord said

to him, "But I will be with you, and you shall smite the Midianites as one man." [17]And he said to him, "If now I have found favor with thee, then show me a sign that it is thou who speakest with me. [18]Do not depart from here, I pray thee, until I come to thee, and bring out my present, and set it before thee." And he said, "I will stay till you return."

[19]So Gideon went into his house and prepared a kid, and unleavened cakes from an ephah of flour; the meat he put in a basket, and the broth he put in a pot, and brought them to him under the oak and presented them. [20]And the angel of God said to him, "Take the meat and the unleavened cakes, and put them on this rock, and pour the broth over them." And he did so. [21]Then the angel of the Lord reached out the tip of the staff that was in his hand, and touched the meat and the unleavened cakes; and there sprang up fire from the rock and consumed the flesh and the unleavened cakes; and the angel of the Lord vanished from his sight. [22]Then Gideon perceived that he was the angel of the Lord; and Gideon said, "Alas, O Lord God! For now I have seen the angel of the Lord face to face." [23]But the Lord said to him, "Peace be to you; do not fear, you shall not die." [24]Then Gideon built an altar there to the Lord, and called it, The Lord is peace. To this day it still stands at Ophrah, which belongs to the Abiezrites.

Here begins the pre-Deuteronomistic narrative about Gideon. Actually the text as it now stands seems to be a composite of two different stories. A narrative about the establishment of a Yahwistic shrine at Ophrah (vv. 11a, 18-24) frames the call of Gideon to be a military leader (vv. 11b-17). Originally these stories circulated among Gideon's own people, the Abiezer clan of Manasseh, before they acquired an "all Israel" meaning with the emergence of a sense of unity among the tribes.

The oak of Ophrah which belonged to Gideon's father was probably an oracular site associated with the worship of

Baal (*cf.*, 6:25-32). Divine/human communication by means of various mantic techniques was an important aspect of ancient Near Eastern religion and is a prominent feature of Gideon's story. The apparition of the Lord's angel (v. 11) and of the Lord as well (v. 14) at the site made it possible for Ophrah to be converted into a Yahwistic cult center. Since the shrine had been a center for the worship of Baal, Gideon is quite slow in recognizing the presence of Yahweh there.

The narrative implies that the Midianite domination of Israel was so complete that the people were reduced to acts of passive resistance. No capable leader such as Othniel or Deborah emerged from the ranks of the tribes. The Lord had to go about the people to search one out. Gideon's reply to the angel's greeting underscores how Israel had come to accept the Midianite domination (vv. 12-13). The Midianites are a fact of life; Yahweh is no longer part of Israel's reality. Gideon's words betray no awareness of the prophetic explanation of Israel's plight which was given in vv. 7-10. This is an indication that the prophetic indictment was introduced at some later time.

Though the Lord does choose Gideon for the mission of liberating Israel from the Midianites (v. 14), Gideon's response is to assert his inadequacy for the mission (v. 15). Such a response is a product of the Deuteronomist who sees Israel's future solely in the hands of God. That future is not dependent in any way upon the nation's own potential or achievements.

The story of Gideon's call ends with a request for a proof — a conclusive sign of the authority with which Gideon is to take up his mission. The sign is cultic in nature. With the giving of the sign, the angel disappears since the action (v. 21) goes beyond the capabilities of the human form which had been assumed in order to speak with Gideon. Fear envelopes Gideon once he realized just who has been speaking with him. This encounter with Yahweh and its significance for Israel was memorialized at Ophrah which became a place of Yahwistic worship under Gideon.

Gideon's Yahwistic credentials
6:25-32

25That night the Lord said to him, "Take your father's bull, the second bull seven years old, and pull down the altar of Baal which your father has, and cut down the Asherah that is beside it; 26and build an altar to the Lord your God on the top of the stronghold here, with stones laid in due order; then take the second bull, and offer it as a burnt offering with the wood of the Asherah which you shall cut down." 27So Gideon took ten men of his servants, and did as the Lord had told him; but because he was too afraid of his family and the men of the town to do it by day, he did it by night.

28When the men of the town rose early in the morning, behold, the altar of Baal was broken down, and the Asherah beside it was cut down, and the second bull was offered upon the altar which had been built. 29And they said to one another, "Who has done this thing?" And after they had made search and inquired, they said, "Gideon the son of Joash has done this thing." 30Then the men of the town said to Joash, "Bring out your son, that he may die, for he has pulled down the altar of Baal and cut down the Asherah beside it." 31But Joash said to all who were arrayed against him, "Will you contend for Baal? Or will you defend his cause? Whoever contends for him shall be put to death by morning. If he is a god, let him contend for himself, because his altar has been pulled down." 32Therefore on that day he was called Jerubbaal, that is to say, "Let Baal contend against him," because he pulled down his altar.

While Gideon is chosen to take up the fight against the Midianite oppressors, Israel must not forget that the real conflict is not between *Midian* and Israel but rather between *Yahweh* and Israel. The Midianite scourge is just a symptom of the real malady: Israel's infidelity to the Lord. Once Gideon pulls down the altar of Baal and the Ashtarah (vv. 25, 27), his most difficult task is completed and the victory over

Midian is assured. This text reflects the prophetic concern that Israel understand the true cause of her problems. The external enemy (Midian) was simply the punishment for Israel's internal sin (apostasy).

Gideon's zeal for Yahweh makes it possible to introduce his Baalistic name, Jerubbaal, without causing a scandal. Gideon's act of destroying the altar of Baal made it possible to give an "orthodox" etymology to that Baalistic name which no doubt was somewhat of an embarrassment to conservative Yahwists like the Deuteronomistic author.

The tribal levies
6:33-35

33Then all the Midianites and the Amalekites and the people of the East came together, and crossing the Jordan they encamped in the Valley of Jezreel. 34But the Spirit of the Lord took possession of Gideon; and he sounded the trumpet and the Abiezrites were called out to follow him. 35And he sent messengers throughout all Manasseh; and they too were called out to follow him. And he sent messengers to Asher, Zebulun and Naphtali; and they went up to meet them.

Once Gideon is designated by God as a leader through the charisma of the Spirit (v. 34), a Holy War against the Midianites begins. Such a war is fought by the tribal levies which now answer Gideon's call. Passive resistance is replaced by Holy War.

Another test
6:36-40

36Then Gideon said to God, "If thou wilt deliver Israel by my hand, as thou hast said, 37behold, I am laying a fleece of wool on the threshing floor; if there is dew on the fleece alone, and it is dry on all the ground, then I shall know that thou wilt deliver Israel by my hand, as thou hast said." 38And it was so. When he rose early next morning and squeezed the fleece, he wrung enough dew from the fleece to fill a bowl with water. [39]Then Gideon said to God, "Let not thy anger burn against me, let me speak but this once; pray, let me make trial only this once with the fleece; pray, let it be dry only on the fleece, and on all the ground let there be dew." [40]And God did so that night; for it was dry on the fleece only, and on all the ground there was dew.

The Gideon story is replete with tests. Gideon asked for proof that he indeed spoke with an angel (6:17). Joash assumed that the destruction of his Baalistic altar will move Baal to prove his divinity (6:31-32). The Lord will use a test to thin out Gideon's army (7:1-8). A dream of a Midianite soldier becomes the answer to another request of Gideon for assurance (7:9-15). The elders of Succoth will help only those military forces which have proven their worth through victory in battle (8:4-9).

The tests with the fleece fit well within this pattern of determining the divine will through signs. It is not unusual for omens to be sought before a battle. This was common enough in the ancient Near East. It is unusual for such techniques to be reported of an Israelite to whom divination was forbidden (Deut 18:9-14). Even though divination may have been quite popular among the populace, still employment of mantic techniques ought not to have been reported of a person just credited with striking a decisive blow for Yahwism. This concern of Gideon to insure the success of his venture even through use of forbidden techniques does suit the purpose of the Deuteronomist who wishes to portray the victory over Midian as the Lord's doing. The repeated requests for signs does serve to build up an element of suspence in the readers. If Gideon is not really convinced of success, how can it come? The answer, of course, is that the Lord gives the victory.

The battle west of the Jordan
7:1—8:3

The army of Israel
7:1-8

7 Then Jerubbaal (that is, Gideon) and all the people who were with him rose early and encamped beside the spring of Harod; and the camp of Midian was north of them, by the hill of Moreh, in the valley.

²The Lord said to Gideon, "The people with you are too many for me to give the Midianites into their hand, lest Israel vaunt themselves against me, saying 'My own hand has delivered me.' ³Now therefore proclaim in the ears of the people, saying, 'Whoever is fearful and trembling, let him return home,'" And Gideon tested them; twenty-two thousand returned, and ten thousand remained.

⁴And the Lord said to Gideon, "The people are still too many; take them down to the water and I will test them for you there; and he of whom I say to you, 'This man shall go with you,' shall go with you; and any of whom I say to you, 'This man shall not go with you,' shall not go."
⁵So he brought the people down to the water; and the Lord said to Gideon, "Every one that laps the water with his tongue, as a dog laps, you shall set by himself; likewise every one that kneels down to drink." ⁶And the number of those that lapped, putting their hands to their mouths, was three hundred men; but all the rest of the people knelt down to drink water. ⁷And the Lord said to Gideon, "With the three hundred men that lapped I will deliver you, and give the Midianites into your hand; and let all the others go every man to his home." ⁸So he took the jars of the people from their hands, and their trumpets; and he sent all the rest of Israel every man to his tent, but retained the three hundred men; and the camp of Midian was below him in the valley.

Whatever the historical situation behind the reduction of

the tribal levies, it served the Deuteronomist's perspective perfectly. The conflict between Israel and Midian was, after all, determined by the conflict between Yahweh and Israel. With Gideon's destruction of the Baalistic altar at Ophrah the latter conflict was settled. Now the Lord became the opponent of Midian. The reduction of the Israelite army to the 300 men supplied by Gideon's own clan (*cf.*, 8:2) served to underscore this theological point. When victory over Midian would be achieved, it would be ascribed to the Lord alone.

Ancient tradition did provide for dismissing from the army any whose cowardice might affect the performance of the troops (Deut 20:8). Gideon's army was still too large for the Lord and a second reduction is achieved by means of a test whose meaning is not absolutely clear. The final effect of these two reductions is, however, quite evident. The possibility of crediting the coming victory over Midian to any human prowess is eliminated. A basic feature of Holy War ideology is that victory belongs to God alone. That is why this story has the suggestion for the second reduction of troops coming from God (7:2), who wishes to insure that Israel could never be mistaken about the source of her military victories.

The nightmare
7:9-15

⁹That same night the Lord said to him, "Arise, go down against the camp; for I have given it into your hand. ¹⁰But if you fear to go down, go down to the camp with Purah your servant; ¹¹and you shall hear what they say, and afterward your hands shall be strengthened to go down against the camp." Then he went down with Purah his servant to the outposts of the armed men that were in the camp. ¹²And the Midianites and the Amalekites and all the people of the East lay along the valley like locusts for multitude; and their camels were without number, as the sand which is upon the seashore for multitude. ¹³When Gideon came, behold, a man was telling a dream to his

comrade; and he said, "Behold, I dreamed a dream; and lo, a cake of barley bread tumbled into the camp of Midian, and came to the tent, and struck it so that it fell, and turned it upside down, so that the tent lay flat." [14]And his comrade answered, "This is no other than the sword of Gideon the son of Joash, a man of Israel; into his hand God has given Midian and all the host."

[15]When Gideon heard the telling of the dream and its interpretation, he worshipped; and he returned to the camp of Israel, and said, "Arise; for the Lord has given the host of Midian into your hand."

The Deuteronomist finds another element of the tradition about Gideon which is well suited to making the point that it is the Lord who brings Israel victory. Gideon and a companion are reassured about the outcome of the imminent battle once they hear a Midianite soldier telling a comrade about a nightmare which he just had. For the Midianite the significance of his dream was obvious: Gideon and his troops would overrun the Midianite camp. In the ancient Near East dreams were considered a vehicle of divine-human communication. The phantasma, if rightly interpreted, provide an infallible guide to the divine ordering of the future.

In the vision the barley loaf represents the agrarian culture of Israel, while the tent points to the nomadic Midianite culture. The crushing of the tent by the barley loaf has only one meaning. The army has been chosen. The general has been assured of victory. All that remains is the battle itself. The scene has been set for the Lord's victory.

The battle
7:16-22

[16]And he divided the three hundred men into three companies, and put trumpets into the hands of all of them and empty jars, with torches inside the jars. [17]And he said to them, "Look at me, and do likewise; when I come to the outskirts of the camp, do as I do. [18]When I blow the trumpet, I and all who are with me, then blow the

trumpets also on every side of all the camp, and shout, 'For the Lord and for Gideon.' "

[19]So Gideon and the hundred men who were with him came to the outskirts of the camp at the beginning of the middle watch, when they had just set the watch; and they blew the trumpets and smashed the jars that were in their hands. [20]And the three companies blew the trumpets and broke the jars, holding in their left hands the torches, and in their right hands the trumpets to blow; and they cried, "A sword for the Lord and for Gideon!" [21]They stood every man in his place round about the camp, and all the army ran; they cried out and fled. [22]When they blew the three hundred trumpets, the Lord set every man's sword against his fellow and against all the army; and the army fled as far as Bethshittah toward Zererah, as far as the border of Abelmeholah, by Tabbath.

While the army of Gideon was not required to do anything in terms of actual combat in order to secure a victory over Midian, the troops were required to perform tasks which would challenge the agility of the most capable. While blowing their battle horns, the soldiers had to break jars which contained lighted torches. They had to sound their horns, hold their lamps and also manage to let out a battle cry — a quite improbable scene.

In all likelihood, the Gideon tradition contained the story of a maneuver in which the Abiezrite force was able to surround the Midianite camp at night without being detected since their torches were hidden within large ceramic jars. Once the troops surrounded the camp of the enemy, they suddenly exposed their presence with the torches and battle cries. The startled enemy was driven into a suicidal panic. This ancient story is later given a slight liturgical tint with the introduction of the trumpets which is reminiscent of the Jericho story (Josh 6). The effect is to transform an old tale of an Abiezrite tactical surprise into an affirmation of faith which gives the Lord full credit for the victory over the Midianites.

The victory is consolidated
7:23—8:3

23And the men of Israel were called out from Naphtali and from Asher and from all Manasseh, and they pursued after Midian.

24And Gideon sent messengers throughout all the hill country of Ephraim, saying, "Come down against the Midianites and seize the waters against them, as far as Bethbarah, and also the Jordan." So all the men of Ephraim were called out, and they seized the waters as far as Bethbarah, and also the Jordan. 25And they took the two princes of Midian, Oreb and Zeeb; they killed Oreb at the rock of Oreb, and Zeeb they killed at the wine press of Zeeb, as they pursued Midian; and they brought the heads of Oreb and Zeeb to Gideon beyond the Jordan. 8 And the men of Ephraim said to him, "What is this that you have done to us, not to call us when you went to fight with Midian?" And they upbraided him violently. 2And he said to them, "What have I done now in comparison with you? Is not the gleaning of the grapes of Ephraim better than the vintage of Abiezer? 3God has given into your hands the princes of Midian, Oreb and Zeeb; what have I been able to do in comparison with you?" Then their anger against him was abated, when he had said this.

Once the Israelite tribes achieved a sense of identity, what were originally local traditions had to be transformed into "all-Israel" traditions in keeping with the new sense of unity which emerged among the diverse worshippers of Yahweh. Sometimes this transformation was done well; other times it was a bit strained. This text is an example of the latter. The scene describes a recall of the troops which Gideon had previously dismissed. From a military perspective it is a highly improbable situation, but it does serve to underscore the importance of Ephraim which did become a dominant force among the central and northern tribes.

The battle east of the Jordan
8:4-35

The pursuit of the Midianites
8:4-12

⁴And Gideon came to the Jordan and passed over, he and the three hundred men who were with him, faint yet pursuing. ⁵So he said to the men of Succoth, "Pray, give loaves of bread to the people who follow me; for they are faint, and I am pursuing after Zebah and Zalmunna, the kings of Midian." ⁶And the officials of Succoth said, "Are Zebah and Zalmunna already in your hand, that we should give bread to your army?" ⁷And Gideon said, "Well then, when the Lord has given Zebah and Zalmunna into my hand, I will flail your flesh with the thorns of the wilderness and with briers." ⁸And from there he went up to Penuel, and spoke to them in the same way; and the men of Penuel answered him as the men of Succoth had answered. ⁹And he said to the men of Penuel, "When I come again in peace, I will break down this tower."

¹⁰Now Zebah and Zalmunna were in Karkor with their army, about fifteen thousand men, all who were left of the army of the people of the East; for there had fallen a hundred and twenty thousand men who drew the sword. ¹¹And Gideon went up by the caravan route east of Nobah and Jogbehah, and attacked the army; for the army was off its guard. ¹²And Zebah and Zalmunna fled; and he pursued them and took the two kings of Midian, Zebah and Zalmunna, and he threw all the army into a panic.

Not only does the scene of the battle change but the character of the protagonists changes as well. First of all, the Lord recedes into the background. True, Gideon does mention the Lord by name twice (vv. 7 and 19) but the reader does not sense any theological concern here which is in any way similar to that of chaps. 6 and 7. The fighting does not represent Yahweh's war but is one of personal revenge. Similarly Gideon is no longer the simple Abiezrite farmer. He becomes an imposing military leader who is offered royal status by his army.

In this section, Gideon eliminates the Midianite threat to his clan by pursuing the enemy, capturing two "kings" of Midian and routing their army. In the course of this pursuit, Gideon is refused help from the elders of Succoth who do not wish to provide support to an army which has not proven itself. (Evidently this tradition is unaware of the battle described in 7:16-22.) The focus on Gideon in this episode points to its antiquity. The text is an ancient saga from the Abiezrite clan which extols the accomplishment of its most famous hero. There is no trace of any theological revision here at all.

Gideon's revenge
8:13-21

13Then Gideon the son of Joash returned from the battle by the ascent of Heres. 14And he caught a young man of Succoth, and questioned him; and he wrote down for him the officials and elders of Succoth, seventy-seven men. 15And he came to the men of Succoth, and said, "Behold Zebah and Zalmunna, about whom you taunted me, saying, 'Are Zebah and Zalmunna already in your hand, that we should give bread to your men who are faint?'" 16And he took the elders of the city and he took thorns of the wilderness and briers and with them taught the men of Succoth. 17And he broke down the tower of Penuel, and slew the men of the city.

18Then he said to Zebah and Zalmunna, "Where are the men whom you slew at Tabor?" They answered, "As you are, so were they, every one of them; they resembled the sons of a king." 19And he said, "They were my brothers, the sons of my mother; as the Lord lives, if you had saved them alive, I would not slay you." 20And he said to Jether his firstborn, "Rise, and slay them." But the youth did not draw his sword; for he was afraid, because he was still a youth. [21]Then Zebah and Zalmunna said, "Rise yourself, and fall upon us; for as the man is, so is his strength." And Gideon arose and slew Zebah and Zalmunna; and he took the crescents that were on the necks of their camels.

The reprisals taken by Gideon against the towns which refused to supply his army are harsh but typical of victor's justice. The stature of Gideon, the folk-hero, grows as he is shown to overpower his immediate enemy as well as any one would ally themselves with the Midianites or even aid their cause albeit indirectly. The second act of reprisal (vv. 18-21) is even more revealing. Here it becomes clear that the reason for Gideon's move against the Midianites was to avenge the death of his brothers. While neither the brothers nor the circumstances of their death are described in any detail, it is clear that the picture of Gideon presented here does not jibe with that of chap. 6. The words exchanged between Gideon and the two kings reflect the insane logic of blood feuds.

It is obvious that in this folk saga there is little theological or moral concern except the unspoken assumption that the God of Israel guides the destiny of nations, tribes and individuals in a marvelous way so as to insure that the divine purpose is served no matter what the intention of the human participants in these events may be. This is a profound belief and it underlies the entire Deuteronomistic History. Such a belief was the one source of hope for the exiles.

The epilogue
8:22-35

[22]Then the men of Israel said to Gideon, "Rule over us, you and your son and your grandson also; for you have delivered us out of the hand of Midian." [23]Gideon said to them, "I will not rule over you, and my son will not rule over you; the Lord will rule over you." [24]And Gideon said to them, "Let me make a request of you; give me every man of you the earrings of his spoil." (For they had golden earrings, because they were Ishmaelites.) [25]And they answered, "We will willingly give them." And they

spread a garment, and every man cast in it the earrings of his spoil. [26]And the weight of the golden earrings that he requested was one thousand seven hundred shekels of gold; besides the crescents and the pendants and the purple garments worn by the kings of Midian, and besides the collars that were about the necks of their camels. [27]And Gideon made an ephod of it and put it in his city, in Ophrah; and all Israel played the harlot after it there, and it became a snare to Gideon and to his family. [28]So Midian was subdued before the people of Israel, and they lifted up their heads no more. And the land had rest forty years in the days of Gideon.

[29]Jerubbaal the son of Joash went and dwelt in his own house. [30]Now Gideon had seventy sons, his own offspring, for he had many wives. [31]And his concubine who was in Shechem also bore him a son, and he called his name Abimelech. [32]And Gideon the son of Joash died in a good old age, and was buried in the tomb of Joash his father, at Ophrah of the Abiezrites.

[33]As soon as Gideon died, the people of Israel turned again and played the harlot after the Baals and made Baalberith their god. [34]And the people of Israel did not remember the Lord their God, who had rescued them from the hand of all their enemies on every side; [35]and they did not show kindness to the family of Jerubbaal (that is, Gideon) in return for all the good that he had done to Israel.

The story of Gideon ends in typical Deuteronomistic fashion, Israel who has been freed from the threats posed by the Midianites is now ready to return to her familiar faults (v. 34). Israel once again failed to learn from her experience. A striking feature of this text is the quite dramatic refusal of the crown by Gideon (v. 23). This refusal may indeed reflect the early Israelite belief that only Yahweh was to reign over Israel or it may reflect a later unhappy experience with the monarchic system which served to confirm the validity of the early practice of denying royal prerogatives to any human lord and ascribing them to Yahweh alone.

The epilogue also contains a repudiation of the ephod which was associated with divinatory rituals at Ophrah. The Deuteronomic tradition was adamant in its repudiation of manticism in any form (Deut 18:9-14). The ephod of Gideon became a means whereby Israel demonstrated her disloyalty to Yahweh and her tendency to become involved with the religious practices of the nations. The ephod had to be condemned.

The story of Gideon is a curious mixture of folklore and theological revision. The Abiezrite clan of Manasseh treasured the tales of its most renowned son. With the development of an Israelite identity among the various groups that worshipped Yahweh, Gideon became a hero for all Israel. He took his place among a succession of heroes whose victories are believed to be signs of the Lord's compassion on a people who are slow to learn the meaning of fidelity. The Deuteronomist tells the story of Gideon one more time in the hope that the Exile is not the end of Israel's story.

ABIMELECH, THE KING
9:1-57

The story of Abimelech serves as the centerpiece of the Deuteronomistic narrative about the period of the Judges even though Abimelech himself is not a judge. The attention paid to Abimelech and the position of his story in the entire narrative of this period are quite significant for determining the theological perspectives that dominated the final draft of not only the Book of Judges but also the Deuteronomistic History as a whole. In addition, the story is significant for some of the historical and political data it provides the reader.

The narrative can be summarized briefly as follows: Abimelech, a son of Gideon/Jerubbaal, first murders his half-brothers and then assumes royal status at Shechem with the assent of that city's popular assembly. When there is a falling out between Abimelech and the assembly, there follows a revolution against his authority. While Abimelech crushes the revolution with great ferocity, he himself is killed.

The political wrangling between the king and the popular assembly is typical of the conflicts that inevitably arise between the centralizing tendencies of a monarchy and the attempts to retain the autonomy of the popular assembly. Ancient Near Eastern texts show that similar struggles took place in other Canaanite city-states. The assembly which confirmed Abimelech's position as king considered its prerogatives to include the right to depose a king not to its liking. Of course, Abimelech challenged the right of the assembly to withdraw its initial support for him as king.

The site of the conflict is Shechem which had been an important Canaanite city-state since the Middle Bronze Age (2200-1550 B.C.). Its position at the pass between Mts. Ebal and Gerezim enabled it to dominate the commerce of central Palestine. The flow of trade that passed through it became the basis of the city's prosperity. Apparently Shechem did not resist the Israelite influx that took place during the 13th century century B.C. and was peacefully integrated into the Yahwistic system. Archaeology finds no evidence for any destruction during the settlement period and the Bible does not mention any campaign against the city while both Deut 27 and Josh 24 portray Shechem as an important cultic center for the Israelite tribes.

The adventures of Abimelech begin after Israel had returned to the service of the Baals (8:23). Once Yahweh is replaced by Baal, it is only a matter of time before the Lord is replaced as king as well. The story of Abimelech shows what happens when just one city of the Yahwistic federation establishes a monarchy. From a theological point of view, Shechem separated itself from the Israelite tribes by establishing a monarchy and thereby it removed Yahweh as king. This centerpiece of the Book of Judges dramatizes the tragedy of rejecting Yahweh as Israel's only king.

Abimelech acquires a throne
9:1-6

9 Now Abimelech the son of Jerubbaal went to Shechem to his mother's kinsmen and said to them and to the whole clan of his mother's family, ²"Say in the ears of all the citizens of Shechem, 'Which is better for you, that all seventy of the sons of Jerubbaal rule over you, or that one rule over you?' Remember also that I am your bone and your flesh." ³And his mother's kinsmen spoke all these words on his behalf in the ears of all the men of Shechem; and their hearts inclined to follow Abimelech, for they said, "He is our brother." ⁴And they gave him seventy pieces of silver out of the house of Baalberith with which Abimelech hired worthless and reckless fellows, who followed him. ⁵And he went to his father's house at Ophrah and slew his brothers the sons of Jerubbaal, seventy men, upon one stone; but Jotham the youngest son of Jerubbaal was left, for he hid himself. ⁶And all the citizens of Shechem came together, and all Bethmillo, and they went and made Abimelech king, by the oak of the pillar at Shechem.

The integration of Shechem into the Israelite system could not have been without some tension and discontent on the part of its leadership class. Apparently Abimelech was able to play on this dissatisfaction in order to thrust himself into a position of accepting an offer of the city's crown from its popular assembly. Gideon's sons were in a position to dominate the whole of central Palestine including Shechem because of their father's victories over Midian. While Abimelech too was a son of Gideon, his mother was from Shechem and apparently his kinship ties were not with his father's clan but with Shechem. Through intermediaries Abimelech was able to convince the city's popular assembly that he was the one to lead their resistance against the dominance of Gideon's clan.

The assembly gives Abimelech the means to collect a mercenary army to carry out the rebellion. The assassination of Gideon's sons "upon one stone" probably reflects a ritual-like action which was to demonstrate the change in power effected by the success of Abimelech's rebellion. With the Israelite rulers eliminated, the assembly of Shechem made Abimelech, the native son, the city's king. While no text ever calls Abimelech "king of Israel," clearly this text is used as a case-study of how the monarchic system works and as such it is an indirect but effective polemic against Israel's monarchy.

Jotham's fable
9:7-15

7When it was told to Jotham, he went and stood on the top of Mount Gerizim, and cried aloud and said to them, "Listen to me, you men of Shechem, that God may listen to you. 8The trees once went forth to anoint a king over them; and they said to the olive tree, 'Reign over us.' 9But the olive tree said to them, 'Shall I leave my fatness, by which gods and men are honored, and go to sway over the trees?' 10And the trees said to the fig tree, 'Come you, and reign over us.' 11But the fig tree said to them, 'Shall I leave my sweetness and my good fruit, and go to sway over the trees?' 12And the trees said to the vine, 'Come you, and reign over us.' 13But the vine said to them, 'Shall I leave my wine which cheers gods and men, and go to sway over the trees?' 14Then all the trees said to the bramble, 'Come you, and reign over us.' 15And the bramble said to the trees, 'If in good faith you are anointing me king over you, then come and take refuge in my shade; but if not, let fire come out of the bramble and devour the cedars of Lebanon.'

According to 9:5, one of Gideon's sons, Jotham by name, escaped the massacre perpetrated by Abimelech and his mercenaries. The following poetic diatribe on the monarchy is fittingly and effectively put on his lips.

There are similar fables in the collection of ancient Near Eastern sapiential literature. In those fables, the institution of the monarchy is assumed to be of divine origin. The characters in the fables then debate about their respective qualifications for the office of king. In the Israelite fable, no such divine origin for the monarchy is assumed and only the least productive element of society seems to be interested in being king.

The point of the fable is quite obvious: the monarchy is at best a worthless institution and at worst a dangerous one. The point is made in v. 15 after every fruitful and productive tree refused the crown. The bramble steps forwards and invites all to take refuge in its shade when, in fact, it is completely useless as a shade tree. On the contrary, destruction is what it really offers, since even the mighty cedars of Lebanon are consumed in the fires which are so quickly spread by its dry vegetation. The attempt to replace Yahweh as king with a human being will travel the same destructive route. The least productive and qualified will present themselves as candidates for the crown. What is worse is that the search for security through the establishment of the monarchy will end by destroying the very security so eagerly sought in human, political terms.

It is hard to see this text as anything but an outright rejection of the monarchy in principle. The placement of this fable within the story of Abimelech makes the theological thrust of the story painfully clear. Its insertion here probably dates from the final, exilic edition of the Deuteronomistic History which placed little faith in the monarchy as a means to secure Israel's future. In the opinion of the final editor, the only way Israel could look confidently toward the future is through obedience to the written authoritative law, *i.e.,* the Book of Deuteronomy. Obedience to the will of the Lord as it is expressed in the law is Israel's only hope.

The revolution against Abimelech
9:22-29

22Abimelech ruled over Israel three years. 23And God sent an evil spirit between Abimelech and the men of

Shechem; and the men of Shechem dealt treacherously with Abimelech; 24that the violence done to the seventy sons of Jerubbaal might come and their blood be laid upon Abimelech their brother, who slew them, and upon the men of Shechem, who strengthened his hands to slay his brothers. 25And the men of Shechem put men in ambush against him on the mountain tops, and they robbed all who passed by them along that way; and it was told Abimelech.

26And Gaal the son of Ebed moved into Shechem with his kinsmen; and the men of Shechem put confidence in him. 27And they went out into the field, and gathered the grapes from their vineyards and trod them, and held festival, and went into the house of their god, and ate and drank and reviled Abimelech. 28And Gaal the son of Ebed said, "Who is Abimelech, and who are we of Shechem, that we should serve him? Did not the son of Jerubbaal and Zebul his officer serve the men of Hamor the father of Shechem? Why then should we serve him? 29Would that this people were under my hand! then I would remove Abimelech. I would say to Abimelech, 'Increase your army, and come out.'"

After a brief chronological note that may indicate that Abimelech had some leadership role among the Israelite tribes in addition to his royal position at Shechem, the Deuteronomist provides the reader with a key to interpreting the rest of the Abimelech story. While there were genuine political problems that arose between Abimelech and the assembly of Shechem, the "real" reason for his downfall was the evil spirit which God sends to disturb the harmony between the king of Shechem and his subjects (v. 23). This same technique is used to explain the fall of Saul (1 Sam 16:14; 18:10) and the false oracles of the prophets consulted by Ahab (1 Kgs 22:21). The reasons for this divine interference is to guarantee that Abimelech's sin of fratricide does catch up with him (v. 24).

Though the Deuteronomist has provided the reader with

the "real" reason for Abimelech's eventual fall, the narrative describes the political events that led to his demise. The conflict between the assembly and Abimelech began with Abimelech's taking exception to the attacks authorized by the assembly against the caravans which passed through Shechemite territory (v. 25). If this would go on unchecked, these caravans would avoid Shechem altogether and the tolls Abimelech collected from them would cease as well. With the arrival of Gaal (v. 26), the assembly had a rival to pit against Abimelech.

The assembly quickly moved to full-scale rebellion. Gaal's rhetoric in encouraging the rebellion is blatantly nationalistic. The effect of Gaal's rival leadership was to pull Shechem out of the Israelite circle. First the assembly rejected the 70 sons of Gideon in favor of Abimelech because he was at least a Shechemite on his mother's side. Now not even that is good enough. The half-Israelite Abimelech is not worthy to rule over the "men of Hamor" (v. 28).

Abimelech's campaigns against Shechem
9:30-45

[30]When Zebul the ruler of the city heard the words of Gaal the son of Ebed, his anger was kindled. [31]And he sent messengers to Abimelech at Arumah, saying, "Behold, Gaal the son of Ebed and his kinsmen have come to Shechem, and they are stirring up the city against you. [32]Now therefore, go by night, you and the men that are with you, and lie in wait in the fields. [33]Then in the morning, as soon as the sun is up, rise early and rush upon the city; and when he and the men that are with him come out against you, you may do to them as occasion offers."

[34]And Abimelech and all the men that were with him rose up by night, and laid wait against Shechem in four companies. [35]And Gaal the son of Ebed went out and stood in the entrance of the gate of the city; and Abimelech and the men that were with him rose from the ambush. [36]And when Gaal saw the men, he said to Zebul,

"Look, men are coming down from the mountain tops!" And Zebul said to him, "You see the shadow of the mountains as if they were men." [37]Gaal spoke again and said, "Look, men are coming down from the center of the land, and one company is coming from the direction of the Diviners' Oak." [38]Then Zebul said to him, "Where is your mouth now, you who said, 'Who is Abimelech, that we should serve him?' Are not these men whom you despised? Go out now and fight with them." [39]And Gaal went out at the head of the men of Shechem, and fought with Abimelech. [40]And Abimelech chased him, and he fled before him; and many fell wounded, up to the entrance of the gate. [41]And Abimelech dwelt at Arumah; and Zebul drove out Gaal and his kinsmen, so that they could not live on at Shechem.

[42]On the following day the men went out into the fields. And Abimelech was told. [43]He took his men and divided them into three companies, and laid wait in the fields; and he looked and saw the men coming out of the city, and he rose against them and slew them. [44]Abimelech and the company that was with him rushed forward and stood at the entrance of the gate of the city, while the two companies rushed upon all who were in the fields and slew them. [45]And Abimelech fought against the city all that day; he took the city, and killed the people that were in it; and he razed the city and sowed it with salt.

There is no overt theological interest in this section. These verses simply describe Abimelech's campaigns against the rebels and their utter defeat. The first battle results in the defeat of the rebel forces under Gaal (v. 40). Abimelech dispatches his general Zebul to follow the retreating army (v. 41). This gives Abimelech a free hand to take his revenge against the city which rejected his rule. This he does with such ferocity that he even sprinkles salt on the city's ruins to signify the utter and irreversible desolation that the rebels have brought upon themselves and their city (v. 45).

The reader, of course, knows that Shechem's mistake was

not the act of rebellion against Abimelech but the act of rebellion against Yahweh. Once the Lord was replaced as king, the destruction of the city was inevitable just as the fall of Jerusalem was the inevitable result of Judah's rejection of Yahweh's rule.

Archaeology has revealed a massive destruction of Shechem during the 12th century B.C. It is quite tempting to associate that destruction with the narrative preserved here.

The end of Abimelech
9:50-57

50Then Abimelech went to Thebez, and encamped against Thebez, and took it. 51But there was a strong tower within the city, and all the people of the city fled to it, all the men and women, and shut themselves in; and they went to the roof of the tower. 52And Abimelech came to the tower, and fought against it, and drew near to the door of the tower to burn it with fire. 53And a certain woman threw an upper millstone upon Abimelech's head, and crushed his skull. 54Then he called hastily to the young man his armor-bearer, and said to him, "Draw your sword and kill me, lest men say of me, 'A woman killed him.'" And his young man thrust him through, and he died. 55And when the men of Israel saw that Abimelech was dead, they departed every man to his home. 56Thus God requited the crime of Abimelech, which he committed against his father in killing his seventy brothers; 57and God also made all the wickedness of the men of Shechem fall back upon their heads, and upon them came the curse of Jotham the son of Jerubbaal.

Abimelech's anger moved him to punish Thebez, one of the village-dependencies of Shechem. In the course of the battle, a woman delivers a mortal blow to the king. To avoid the ignominy of having been killed by a woman, Abimelech asks his armor bearer to administer the *coup de grâce*. Again the reader knows that neither the woman nor Abimelech's servant was responsible for his death. It was just the last act of a terrible drama which Abimelech himself directed. The drama's first act was Abimelech's murder of his own brothers.

This centerpiece of the Book of Judges shows the inevitable consequences of imitating the discredited socio-political system of the Canaanite city-states. Throughout Palestine, Israelite forces were overthrowing that system and replacing it with one based on the Lordship of Yahweh. Once the Lord is rejected and replaced by a human king only disaster results. The implied indictment of the Israelite monarchy is surprising if not shocking. Such an indictment could emerge only after bitter experience and disillusionment with the monarchy. Of course, the Exile was the fact which makes this indictment understandable. It seems obvious that the final editor of the Book of Judges does not look to the monarchy as the key to Israel's future.

THE OTHER JUDGES
10:1-5 and 12:8-15

10 After Abimelech there arose to deliver Israel Tola the son of Puah, son of Dodo, a man of Issachar; and he lived at Shamir in the hill country of Ephraim. ²And he judged Israel twenty-three years. Then he died, and was buried at Shamir.

³After him arose Jair the Gileadite, who judged Israel twenty-two years. ⁴And he had thirty sons who rode on thirty asses; and they had thirty cities, called Havvothjair to this day, which are in the land of Gilead. ⁵And Jair died, and was buried in Kamon.

12 ⁸After him Ibzan of Bethlehem judged Israel. ⁹He had thirty sons; and thirty daughters he gave in marriage outside his clan, and thirty daughters he brought in from outside for his sons. And he judged Israel seven years. ¹⁰Then Ibzan died, and was buried at Bethlehem.

¹¹After him Elon the Zebulunite judged Israel; and he judged Israel ten years. ¹²Then Elon the Zebulunite died,

and was buried at Aijalon in the land of Zebulun.
    ^{13}After him Abdon the son of Hillel the Pirathonite judged Israel. ^{14}He had forty sons and thirty grandsons, who rose on seventy asses; and he judged Israel eight years. ^{15}Then Abdon the son of Hillel the Pirathonite died, and was buried at Pirathon in the land of Ephraim, in the hill country of the Amalekites.

    Six of the judges remembered by Israel have no specific deeds associated with their administration. The reference to the five judges cited in these two texts follows the pattern set by the reference to Shamgar in 3:31: name, tribal origin, length of administration, death and burial. Perhaps these six were added to bring the total number of Judges named in the book to 12. This does reflect the pan-Israelite intention of these narratives.
    The function of these judges cannot be determined from the text with any certainty. Though Tola "arose to save Israel" (10:1), it is not clear from whom. All the others are described as simply judging Israel. Again it is not apparent what this task entailed. That these individuals served in some sort of administrative role is about all that can be concluded. Evidently their service was such that their names were worth remembering. While they may not have led Israel into great battles, they preserved the people from forces that were always threatening the fragile unity of Yahweh's worshippers.

JEPHTHAH
10:6—12:7

    The East-Jordan setting for the Jephthah story is unique in the Book of Judges. The story itself is a masterpiece in holding the reader's attention. The unfolding of the narrative involves a series of crises — as one is resolved, another is introduced. While Israel is saved from the Ammonite threat, the story ends on a tragic note for the protagonist. While his military skill does save Israel, Jephthah experi-

ences personal misfortune as a result of the victory he wins
for Israel.

The Deuteronomistic introduction
10:6-16

6And the people of Israel again did what was evil in the
sight of the Lord, and served the Baals and the Ashtaroth,
the gods of Syria, the gods of Sidon, the gods of Moab,
the gods of the Ammonites, and the gods of the Philistines; and they forsook the Lord, and did not serve him.
7And the anger of the Lord was kindled against Israel,
and he sold them into the hand of the Philistines and into
the hand of the Ammonites, 8and they crushed and
oppressed the children of Israel that year. For eighteen
years they oppressed all the people of Israel that were
beyond the Jordan in the land of the Amorites, which is in
Gilead. 9And the Ammonites crossed the Jordan to fight
also against Judah and against Benjamin and against the
house of Ephraim; so that Israel was sorely distressed.

10And the people of Israel cried to the Lord, saying,
"We have sinned against thee, because we have forsaken
our God and have served the Baals." 11And the Lord said
to the people of Israel, "Did I not deliver you from the
Egyptians and from the Amorites, from the Ammonites
and from the Philistines? 12The Sidonites also, and the
Amalekites, and the Maonites, oppressed you; and you
cried to me, and I delivered you out of their hand. 13Yet
you have forsaken me and served other gods; therefore I
will deliver you no more. 14Go and cry to the gods whom
you have chosen; let them deliver you in the time of your
distress." 15And the people of Israel said to the Lord, "We
have sinned; do to us whatever seems good to thee; only
deliver us, we pray thee, this day." 16So they put away the
foreign gods from among them and served the Lord; and
he became indignant over the misery of Israel.

Too often the Deuteronomist is described as having introduced a cyclical view of Israel's life during the period of the
Judges. While the Deuteronomist does note Israel's ten-

dency towards repeated failures in her commitment to Yahweh and the consequent military and political threats from her neighbors, the purpose is not to describe a recurring pattern of behavior but to insist upon the Lord's compassion. The question underlying this Deuteronomistic presentation is how long could Israel depend on the Lord's mercy. In this introduction to the ancient stories about Jephthah, it is clear that matters are getting worse. First Israel is accused of worshipping a panoply of Canaanite gods. Then there is the conversation between Yahweh and Israel which makes it clear that the Lord's patience is at an end (vv. 13-14). Obviously the simple confession of sin in v. 10 is not enough to return Israel to God's favor. This leads Israel to undertake a real conversion by removing the strange gods and returning to the exclusive service of Yahweh (v. 16a). The meaning of the editorial comment in v. 16b is not completely clear in Hebrew. The most common translations imply that once the conversion takes place, God is now ready to act on Israel's behalf. This ambiguous text may also mean that God was weary of Israel's frantic but ultimately insincere attempts at conversion. In that case, the reader is left to wonder about Israel's future. What will become of her as she faces the enemies which surround her? One element missing from the usual pattern of these Deuteronomistic introductions is the note that God has raised up a judge to deliver Israel. In fact, the text explicitly states that God refused to do so (v. 13). This emphasizes the genuine gravity of Israel's situation.

The choice of Jephthah
10:17—11:11

[17]Then the Ammonites were called to arms, and they encamped in Gilead; and the people of Israel came together, and they encamped at Mizpah. [18]And the people, the leaders of Gilead, said one to another, "Who is the man that will begin to fight against the Ammonites? He shall be head over all the inhabitants of Gilead."

11 Now Jephthah the Gileadite was a mighty warrior,

but he was the son of a harlot. Gilead was the father of Jephthah. 2And Gilead's wife also bore him sons; and when his wife's sons grew up, they thrust Jephthah out, and said to him, "You shall not inherit in our father's house; for you are the son of another woman." 3Then Jephthah fled from his brothers, and dwelt in the land of Tob; and worthless fellows collected around Jephthah, and went raiding with him.

4After a time the Ammonites made war against Israel. 5And when the Ammonites made war against Israel, the elders of Gilead went to bring Jephthah from the land of Tob; 6and they said to Jephthah, "Come and be our leader, that we may fight with the Ammonites." 7But Jephthah said to the elders of Gilead, "Did you not hate me, and drive me out of my father's house? Why have you come to me now when you are in trouble?" 8And the elders of Gilead said to Jephthah, "That is why we have turned to you now, that you may go with us and fight with the Ammonites, and be our head over all the inhabitants of Gilead." 9Jephthah said to the elders of Gilead, "If you bring me home again to fight with the Ammonites, and the Lord gives them over to me, I will be your head." 10And the elders of Gilead said to Jephthah, "The Lord will be witness between us; we will surely do as you say." 11So Jephthah went with the elders of Gilead, and the people made him head and leader over them; and Jephthah spoke all his words before the Lord at Mizpah.

Evidently the leadership of Gilead did not consider the Ammonite problem to have any religious roots at all. They attempt to handle it administratively by simply looking for a competent military leader to deal with the situation. Jephthah received his commission as a military leader only after careful negotiations. The choice of Gilead's elders falls on Jephthah not because he is endowed with the spirit but because he has proven to be a successful military man. While this choice portends the end of the Ammonite hold over Israel, it is just the beginning of Jephthah's problems.

The narrative inspires a certain sympathy for Jephthah. Though he has been unfairly treated by the Gileadites because of the unfortunate circumstances of his birth, Jephthah is not marked by bitterness. He negotiates with his former enemies in good faith and accepts only that power which can be legitimately offered to him — a marked contrast with Abimelech. Unfortunately the offer made by the Gileadites will cost Jephthah dearly. Unlike Yahweh who refuses to accept the offer made by Israel, Jephthah does. Yahweh has heard Israel's promises of fidelity too often to be moved by them. To the social outcast Jephthah the promise of leadership in Gilead was an offer that could not be passed up. Though the choice of Jephthah is described as an administrative judgment on the part of Gilead's elders, the scene does conclude at the sanctuary in Mizpah where Jephthah no doubt went to seal ritually the compact he made with Gilead.

Negotiation with Ammon
11:12-28

[12]Then Jephthah sent messengers to the king of the Ammonites and said, "What have you against me, that you have come to me to fight against my land?" [13]And the king of the Ammonites answered the messengers of Jephthah, "Because Israel on coming from Egypt took away my land, from the Arnon to the Jabbok and to the Jordan; now therefore restore it peaceably." [14]And Jephthah sent messengers again to the king of the Ammonites [15]and said to him, "Thus says Jephthah: Israel did not take away the land of Moab or the land of the Ammonites, [16]but when they came up from Egypt, Israel went through the wilderness to the Red Sea and came to Kadesh. [17]Israel then sent messengers to the king of Edom, saying, 'Let us pass, we pray, through your land'; but the king of Edom would not listen. And they sent also to the king of Moab, but he would not consent. So Israel remained at Kadesh. [18]Then they journeyed through the wilderness, and went around the land of Edom and the

land of Moab, and arrived on the east side of the land of Moab, and camped on the other side of the Arnon; but they did not enter the territory of Moab, for the Arnon was the boundary of Moab. ¹⁹Israel then sent messengers to Sihon king of the Amorites, king of Heshbon; and Israel said to him, 'Let us pass, we pray, through your land to our country.' ²⁰But Sihon did not trust Israel to pass through his territory; so Sihon gathered all his people together, and encamped at Jahaz, and fought with Israel. ²¹And the Lord, the God of Israel, gave Sihon and all his people into the hand of Israel, and they defeated them; so Israel took possession of all the land of the Amorites, who inhabited that country. ²²And they took possession of all the territory of the Amorites from the Arnon to the Jabbok and from the wilderness to the Jordan. ²³So then the Lord, the God of Israel, dispossessed the Amorites from before his people Israel; and are you to take possession of them? ²⁴Will you not possess what Chemosh your god gives you to possess? And all that the Lord our God has dispossessed before us, we will possess. ²⁵Now are you any better than Balak the son of Zippor, king of Moab? Did he ever strive against Israel, or did he ever go to war with them? ²⁶While Israel dwelt in Heshbon and its villages, and in Aroer and its villages, and in all the cities that are on the banks of the Arnon, three hundred years, why did you not recover them within that time? ²⁷I therefore have not sinned against you, and you do me wrong by making war on me; the Lord, the Judge, decide this day between the people of Israel and the people of Ammon." ²⁸But the king of the Ammonites did not heed the message of Jephthah which he sent to him.

The manner in which Jephthah acquired his position as the military leader of Gilead is unique in the Book of Judges as is the method he chose to exercise that office — through negotiation with the enemy. This is the only example of diplomacy as a method of resolving disputes in Judges.

Jephthah tries to mediate the conflict which concerns claims of sovereignty over what had been the territory of Moab. The claims of Israel and the counterclaims of Ammon are based on historical and religious precedents and are a bit confusing as such territorial disputes tend to be. The point made by the Deuteronomist, who is naturally drawn to the Israelite side of the argument, is a mixture of theology and international law. Land is a grant from the gods. Conquest and possession of the land is a sure sign of this divine donation. In effect, the fact of conquest determines the legitimacy of any claim to a particular territory. The Ammonites reject this argument. The negotiations fail and war is inevitable.

Jephthah's vow
11:29-40

[29]Then the Spirit of the Lord came upon Jephthah, and he passed through Gilead and Manasseh, and passed on to Mizpah of Gilead, and from Mizpah of Gilead he passed on to the Ammonites. [30]And Jephthah made a vow to the Lord, and said, "If thou wilt give the Ammonites into my hand, [31]then whoever comes forth from the doors of my house to meet me, when I return victorious from the Ammonites, shall be the Lord's, and I will offer him up for a burnt offering." [32]So Jephthah crossed over to the Ammonites to fight against them; and the Lord gave them into his hand. [33]And he smote them from Aroer to the neighborhood of Minnith, twenty cities, and as far as Abelkeramim, with a very great slaughter. So the Ammonites were subdued before the people of Israel.

[34]Then Jephthah came to his home at Mizpah; and behold, his daughter came out to meet him with timbrels and with dances; she was his only child; beside her he had neither son nor daughter. [35]And when he saw her, he rent his clothes, and said, "Alas, my daughter! you have brought me very low and you have become the cause of great trouble to me; for I have opened my mouth to the Lord, and I cannot take back my vow." [36]And she said to him, "My father, if you have opened your mouth to the

Lord, do to me according to what has gone forth from your mouth, now that the Lord has avenged you on your enemies, on the Ammonites." 37And she said to her father, "Let this thing be done for me; let me alone two months, that I may go and wander on the mountains, and bewail my virginity, I and my companions." 38And he said, "Go." And he sent her away for two months; and she departed, she and her companions, and bewailed her virginity upon the mountains. 39And at the end of two months, she returned to her father, who did with her according to his vow which he had made. She had never known a man. And it became a custom in Israel 40that the daughters of Israel went year by year to lament the daughter of Jephthah the Gileadite four days in the year.

The outcome of the battle with Ammon is almost an aside (vv. 32-33), for the central piece of the Jephthah story is the vow. The narrative of the vow begins with the note that Jephthah did come to be possessed by "the Spirit of the Lord" (v. 29). How or why Jephthah was so endowed is left unsaid. Presumably it was to enable Jephthah to lead Israel to victory over Ammon. The war was a serious undertaking since Ammon was not an enemy easily overcome. Though Ammon would arise again to harass Israel (1 Sam 11; 2 Sam 10; 12), Jephthah's victory at least removed the Ammonite threat in the pre-monarchic period.

The victory is achieved as a result of Jephthah's vow which promises sacrifice in exchange for victory (vv. 30-31). The Hebrew text does not assume that a person would be the first to meet Jephthah upon his return from battle. Given the arrangement of typical Palestinian homes of the period whose courtyards usually housed animals acceptable for sacrifice, it is likely that Jephthah assumed that one of these animals — not his daughter — would be the first to be encountered upon his return. Since his daughter was in fact the first to meet him, Jephthah had to conclude that God wanted her as a sacrificial victim instead of any animal. While human sacrifice is not usually acceptable in Old Testament religion, neither is it unknown (2 Kgs 16:3; Ezek

20:25-26, 31). Here the sacrifice of Jephthah's daughter is not criticized in any way. On the contrary, it is considered as necessary in the fulfillment of the vow which Jephthah made. Vows once made to the Lord must be fulfilled, no matter what the cost.

An additional complication comes with the cultic remembrance of Jephthah's daughter mentioned in v. 39. While similar rites are found with some frequency in the ancient Near East, they are not attested with any sort of approval in the Old Testeament (*cf.,* Ezek 8:14; Zech 12:11). The practice of human sacrifice and that of ritual mourning for the dead reflect the strong influence of Canaanite religious practices upon early Israel. As the Israelite cult achieved an identity independent of its Canaanite roots, these practices are censured and gradually fall into disuse.

A civil war
12:1-7

12 The men of Ephraim were called to arms, and they crossed to Zaphon and said to Jephthah, "Why did you cross over to fight against the Ammonites, and did not call us to go with you? We will burn your house over you with fire." ²And Jephthah said to them, "I and my people had a great feud with the Ammonites; and when I called you, you did not deliver me from their hand. ³And when I saw that you would not deliver me, I took my life in my hand, and crossed over against the Ammonites, and the Lord gave them into my hand; why then have you come up to me this day, to fight against me?" ⁴Then Jephthah gathered all the men of Gilead and fought with Ephraim; and the men of Gilead smote Ephraim, because they said, "You are fugitives of Ephraim, you Gileadites, in the midst of Ephraim and Manasseh." ⁵And the Gileadites took the fords of the Jordan against the Ephraimites. And when any of the fugitives of Ephraim said, "Let me go over," the men of Gilead said to him, "Are you an Ephraimite?" When he said, "No," ⁶they said to him, "Then say Shibboleth," and he said, "Sibboleth," for he could not pronounce it right; then they seized him and slew him at the fords of the Jordan. And there fell at that time forty-two thousand of the Ephraimites.

⁷Jephthah judged Israel six years. Then Jephthah the Gileadite died, and was buried in his city in Gilead.

The Jephthah story ends with still another complication for the hero. The tribe of Ephraim probably claimed a certain position of dominance among the Israelites living in central Palestine. As in the Gideon story (8:1-3), Ephraim is put out because of the independent action of a local leader. Perhaps the basis for Ephraim's objection is that without its participation in the move against the Ammonites, the tribe would have no right to the spoils of war that accrue to the victors. On the other hand, the story may reflect those countless border squabbles that take place for no good reason but which result in the loss of life for both sides in the conflict.

The story contains an interesting vignette about a password used by the Gileadites to identify any Ephraimite who was in retreat after the conflict with Jephthah's troops. Local variations in the pronunciation of a common word (*shibboleth*: ear of grain or water current) aided in the identification.

Once all the battles were complete, Jephthah had a relatively brief term as a judge (v. 7). As usual the Deuteronomist takes note of his death and burial place.

The Jephthah story is a harbinger of the tragedy to come for Israel. God was no longer swayed by Israel's claim of repentance (10:13). This time Israel was fortunate that someone was able to step in the breach during her crisis with the Ammonites. Now that Israel could not depend upon God's compassion, how long could she depend upon luck?

SAMSON
13:1—16:31

The geographical setting for the stories about Samson is the territory which Josh 19:40-46 assigns to the tribe of Dan.

This territory is directly west of Jerusalem and extends to the Mediterranean Sea. The same tradition maintains that Dan was not able to consolidate its hold on that land and had to resettle in the far north of Palestine (*cf.,* Josh 19:47-48; Judg 17-18). The Israelites who first settled in the hills of central Palestine eventually began making tentative forays into the fertile plains which were at the base of those hills to the west. Under such circumstances the Israelite settlers could not avoid conflicts with the people who already occupied those plains — the Philistines. The stories about Samson preserve the memory of those early encounters between the Israelites and the Philistines, the most formidable enemy Israel was to face in her attempt to secure possession of the land of promise.

The Philistines were an Indo-European people whose invasion of the eastern Mediterranean region was probably caused by disruptions in their own homeland. Their efficient political organization, effective military discipline and superiority in arms made it a simple matter for them to exercise hegemony in some of the same territory desired by certain Israelite tribes. Though they introduced some distinctive ceramic artifacts into their new homeland, the Philistines adopted so much of the culture of Canaan that there remains almost no trace of their own language and culture. They were a force to contend with from their arrival in the eastern Mediterranean in 1200 B.C. until the time of David (1000 B.C.). Though they concentrated their presence along the coastal plain, the Philistine domination must have become legendary since a thousand years later the Romans named a portion of their own eastern Mediterranean holdings after them: Palestine.

Samson does not command an Israelite or even a Danite army against the Philistines nor does he inflict the final blow against them. Instead a more modest claim is made by Judg 13:5. Samson simply *began* the struggle against the Philistines. At most Samson can be described as a guerrilla who harassed the Philistines by his ability to foil their plans and inflict some heavy though not crippling blows against them.

The structure of these stories is uncomplicated. After an introduction, which describes Samson's miraculous birth (chap. 13), there follow three stories of his unhappy encounters with women (chaps. 14-16). The pattern of these encounters is always the same. First Samson becomes involved with a woman who is used by the Philistines to entrap Samson. He, in turn, foils the Philistine plans and delivers a devastating defeat upon them. The Philistines are portrayed here as oppressive villains.

The birth of Samson
13:1-25

13   And the people of Israel again did what was evil in the sight of the Lord; and the Lord gave them into the hand of the Philistines for forty years.

²And there was a certain man of Zorah, of the tribe of the Danites, whose name was Manoah; and his wife was barren and had no children. ³And the angel of the Lord appeared to the woman and said to her, "Behold, you are barren and have no children; but you shall conceive and bear a son. ⁴Therefore beware, and drink no wine or strong drink, and eat nothing unclean, ⁵for lo, you shall conceive and bear a son. No razor shall come upon his head, for the boy shall be a Nazirite to God from birth; and he shall begin to deliver Israel from the hand of the Philistines." ⁶Then the woman came and told her husband, "A man of God came to me, and his countenance was like the countenance of the angel of God, very terrible; I did not ask him whence he was, and he did not tell me his name; ⁷but he said to me, 'Behold, you shall conceive and bear a son; so then drink no wine or strong drink, and eat nothing unclean, for the boy shall be a Nazirite to God from birth to the day of his death.'"

⁸Then Manoah entreated the Lord, and said, "O, Lord, I pray thee, let the man of God whom thou didst send come again to us, and teach us what we are to do with the boy that will be born." ⁹And God listened to the voice of Manoah, and the angel of God came again to the

woman as she sat in the field; but Manoah her husband was not with her. [10]And the woman ran in haste and told her husband, "Behold, the man who came to me the other day has appeared to me." [11]And Manoah arose and went after his wife, and came to the man and said to him, "Are you the man who spoke to this woman?" And he said, "I am." [12]And Manoah said, "Now when your words come true, what is to be the boy's manner of life, and what is he to do?" [13]And the angel of the Lord said to Manoah, "Of all that I said to the woman let her beware. [14]She may not eat of anything that comes from the vine, neither let her drink wine or strong drink, or eat any unclean thing; all that I commanded her let her observe."

[15]Manoah said to the angel of the Lord, "Pray, let us detain you, and prepare a kid for you." [16]And the angel of the Lord said to Manoah, "If you detain me, I will not eat of your food; but if you make ready a burnt offering, then offer it to the Lord." (For Manoah did not know that he was the angel of the Lord.) [17]And Manoah said to the angel of the Lord, "What is your name, so that, when your words come true, we may honor you?" [18]And the angel of the Lord said to him, "Why do you ask my name, seeing it is wonderful?" [19]So Manoah took the kid with the cereal offering, and offered it upon the rock to the Lord, to him who works wonders. [20]And when the flame went up toward heaven from the altar, the angel of the Lord ascended in the flame of the altar while Manoah and his wife looked on; and they fell on their faces to the ground.

[21]The angel of the Lord appeared no more to Manoah and to his wife. Then Manoah knew that he was the angel of the Lord. [22]And Manoah said to his wife, "We shall surely die, for we have seen God." [23]But his wife said to him, "If the Lord had meant to kill us, he would not have accepted a burnt offering and a cereal offering at our hands, or shown us all these things, or now announced to us such things as these." [24]And the woman bore a son, and called his name Samson; and the boy grew, and the Lord

blessed him. ²⁵And the Spirit of the Lord began to stir him in Mahanehdan, between Zorah and Eshtaol.

The Deuteronomistic introduction is quite minimal here (v. 1). The main thrust of this introduction to Samson's career seems to be an effort to authenticate Samson as a genuine judge since it is not clear at first how such an individual as Samson could be considered a judge. Not only was Samson not a pious worshipper of Yahweh, he was one to ignore the vows which bound him as a Nazirite and he even married foreign women. No Israelites are associated with Samson either during his selection to or execution of the judicial office. How could such a person be numbered among the likes of Deborah, Barak and Gideon?

The story of the wonders surrounding the birth of Samson begins with the note that his mother had been "barren and childless" (vv. 2-3). The barren woman as the mother of an important child is a familiar motif in Biblical literature: Sarah/Isaac (Gen 18:9-15); Rebecca/Jacob (Gen 25:21-26); Rachel/Joseph (Gen 29:31; 30:22-24) and Hannah/Samuel (1 Sam 1:2, 19-20). Another indication of the child's future greatness is given by the angel who announces his birth. Again this is reminiscent of the episode about the three "men" who visit Abraham and Sarah to predict the birth of Isaac (Gen 18).

The angel tells the wife of Manoah that the son she will conceive and bear is to be a Nazirite. The special observances associated with the Nazirites are given in Num 6:1-21. The Nazirites appear to have been militant and conservative religionists who tried to reproduce the life style associated with early Yahwism. While Num 6 assumes that keeping the Nazirite vows is a temporary condition, this text and Amos 2:11-12 appear to imply that the Nazirite life style was to be permanent. The Deuteronomistic view of the Nazirite vows associates these with the ritual purity required of those who would fight the battles of Yahweh (13:5 and Deut 29:6). Since Samson was a Nazirite from birth, his conflicts with the Philistines become the battles of Yahweh.

The note (v. 5) that Samson merely began the move against the Philistines reflects the historical fact that the power of the Philistines was not broken until the time of David. Whatever success Samson achieved was clearly limited in scope.

The parents of Samson are depicted as pious Israelites who wish to be certain that they understand the divine will so that they may be in a position to be obedient to it. This contrasts sharply with the future behavior of their son. The encounter of Minoah and his wife with the angel in vv. 6-23 follows a sequence similar to that of Gideon's encounter with an angel in 6:11-23. First there is a divine message (vv. 13-14) which is followed by an offer of food. The food is used for a sacrifice (vv. 15-19). The scene concludes with the reassurance that comes from faith (vv. 15-19). Notice that it is the woman who displays the faith which discerned the favorable attitude of God toward her and her husband.

This episode concludes with the note that the "spirit of the Lord" took possession of Samson (v. 25). This implies that Samson the Nazirite is distinct from Samson the charismatic. The only effect that the Spirit of the Lord seems to have in Samson's life is the great physical strength it gives him (14:6, 19; 15:14). Sometimes, however, his strength seems to exist without the Spirit (16:3, 38) and at still other times it depends upon his being a Nazirite (16:17). The picture drawn of Samson in these chapters is not a rigidly consistent one. This does not eliminate their historical value entirely since Samson could not have been arbitrarily put forward as a judge were there not some basis in Israel's collective memory of her leaders in the pre-monarchic period.

Samson's Wedding
14:1-20

14 Samson went down to Timnah, and at Timnah he saw one of the daughters of the Philistines. ²Then he came up, and told his father and mother, "I saw one of the daughters of the Philistines at Timnah; now get her for me as my wife." ³But his father and mother said to him, "Is there not a woman among the daughters of your kinsmen, or among all our people, that you must go to take a wife from the uncircumcised Philistines?" But Samson said to his father, "Get her for me; for she pleases me well."

⁴His father and mother did not know that it was from the Lord; for he was seeking an occasion against the Philistines. At that time the Philistines had dominion over Israel.

⁵Then Samson went down with his father and mother to Timnah, and he came to the vineyards of Timnah. And behold, a young lion roared against him; ⁶and the Spirit of the Lord came mightily upon him, and he tore the lion asunder as one tears a kid; and he had nothing in his hand. But he did not tell his father or his mother what he had done. ⁷Then he went down and talked with the woman; and she pleased Samson well. ⁸And after a while he returned to take her; and he turned aside to see the carcass of the lion, and behold, there was a swarm of bees in the body of the lion, and honey. ⁹He scraped it out into his hands, and went on, eating as he went; and he came to his father and mother, and gave some to them, and they ate. But he did not tell them that he had taken the honey from the carcass of the lion.

¹⁰And his father went down to the woman, and Samson made a feast there; for so the young men used to do. ¹¹And when the people saw him, they brought thirty companions to be with him. ¹²And Samson said to them, "Let me now put a riddle to you; if you can tell me what it is, within the seven days of the feast, and find it out, then I will give you thirty linen garments and thirty festal garments; ¹³but if you cannot tell me what it is, then you shall give me thirty linen garments and thirty festal garments." And they said to him, "Put your riddle, that we may hear it." ¹⁴And he said to them,

"Out of the eater came something to eat.

Out of the strong came something sweet."

And they could not in three days tell what the riddle was.

¹⁵On the fourth day they said to Samson's wife, "Entice

your husband to tell us what the riddle is, lest we burn you and your father's house with fire. Have you invited us here, to impoverish us?" 16And Samson's wife wept before him, and said, "You only hate me, you do not love me; you have put a riddle to my countrymen, and you have not told me what it is." And he said to her, "Behold, I have not told my father nor my mother, and shall I tell you?" 17She wept before him the seven days that their feast lasted; and on the seventh day he told her, because she pressed him hard. Then she told the riddle to her countrymen. 18And the men of the city said to him on the seventh day before the sun went down,
"What is sweeter than honey?
  What is stronger than a lion?"
And he said to them,
"If you had not plowed with my heifer,
  you would not have found out my riddle."
19And the Spirit of the Lord came mightily upon him, and he went down to Ashkelon and killed thirty men of the town, and took their spoil and gave the festal garments to those who had told the riddle. In hot anger he went back to his father's house. 20And Samson's wife was given to his companion, who had been his best man.

Samson's character, as it is revealed in the course of his marriage with a Philistine woman, contrasts sharply with the piety of his parents. Samson is simply too headstrong and therefore he cannot recognize his naivete when it comes to women and the potential trouble it can bring him. This naivete becomes Samson's fatal flaw and will eventually bring him down. Samson is simply too quick to be led astray by foreign women who may be attractive but who always mean trouble for Yahwists. This never dawns on Samson even after three disastrous alliances. An even greater example of his naivete is Samson's refusal to believe that he could ever be betrayed by a woman — presumably because they would be so in love with him.

Samson's parents are more realistic. They show the traditional aversion to marriage outside the clan (*cf.,* Gen 24:1-4; 26:34; 27:46—28:9). They refuse to have anything to do with Samson's wife presumably because the marriage with a foreign woman runs contrary to accepted Israelite practice. The editorial note in v. 4 reflects the belief that God can use human folly and sin to accomplish a divine purpose (*cf.,* the Joseph story, Gen 17-50, especially 50:20).

The type of marriage contracted by Samson with his Philistine bride apparently did not involve permanent cohabitation. Evidently the bride remained within her father's household and Samson would make only periodic visits to her (*cf.,* 15:1). The explanatory note in v. 10 was probably necessary since the Israelite readers of this story would have found the whole business connected with this marriage rather unfamiliar and odd. In any case, Samson's marriage with the Philistine woman was just the spark that was needed to ignite the hostility felt between the Israelites and the Philistines — hostility which Samson would have liked to ignore, but in the end could not.

This hostility flares up in the course of the verbal jousting that often takes place in the course of the protracted drinking bouts that are associated with the celebration of a wedding. In the ancient Near East, this jousting sometimes involved proposing and solving riddles. In this case, Samson shows himself to be rather adept at the game. The obvious meaning of his riddle (v. 14) is rather ribald and even obscene, and in the present context it suggests a newly married man's boasting of his sexual potency. In reality, the true meaning of the riddle cannot be ascertained without being aware of the particular reference which is at the basis of the imaged used in the riddle (*cf.,* vv. 5-9). In other words, Samson proposed a riddle that could not be solved. He made a wager that he could not lose — or so he thought. Samson's bride of one week betrayed him and caused him to lose the bet (vv. 16-17). The upshot of the betrayal is to further inflame the hostility of the Philistines since Samson robs the Philistines of Ashkelon to pay those of Timnah (v. 19). Samson did prove himself to be a worthy opponent of the Philistines. Both his brains and his brawn were up to any challenge, but a woman was able to frustrate his purpose.

Samson's revenge
15:1-20

15   After a while, at the time of wheat harvest, Samson went to visit his wife with a kid; and he said, "I will go in to my wife in the chamber." But her father would not allow him to go in. ²And her father said, "I really thought that you utterly hated her; so I gave her to your companion. Is not her younger sister fairer than she? Pray take her instead." ³And Samson said to them, "This time I shall be blameless in regard to the Philistines, when I do them mischief." ⁴So Samson went and caught three hundred foxes, and took torches; and he turned them tail to tail, and put a torch between each pair of tails. ⁵And when he had set fire to the torches, he let the foxes go into the standing grain of the Philistines, and burned up the shocks and the standing grain, as well as the olive orchards. ⁶Then the Philistines said, "Who has done this?" And they said, "Samson, the son-in-law of the Timnite, because he has taken his wife and given her to his companion." And the Philistines came up, and burned her and her father with fire. ⁷And Samson said to them, "If this is what you do, I swear I will be avenged upon you, and after that I will quit." ⁸And he smote them hip and thigh with great slaughter; and he went down and stayed in the cleft of the rock of Etam.

⁹Then the Philistines came up and encamped in Judah, and made a raid on Lehi. ¹⁰And the men of Judah said, "Why have you come up against us?" They said, "We have come up to bind Samson, to do to him as he did to us." ¹¹Then three thousand men of Judah went down to the cleft of the rock of Etam, and said to Samson, "Do you not know that the Philistines are rulers over us?" And he said to them, "As they did to me, so have I done to them." ¹²And they said to him, "We have come down to bind you, that we may give you into the hands of the

Philistines." And Samson said to them, "Swear to me that you will not fall upon me yourselves." [13]They said to him, "No; we will only bind you and give you into their hands; we will not kill you." So they bound him with two new ropes, and brought him up from the rock.

[14]When he came to Lehi, the Philistines came shouting to meet him; and the Spirit of the Lord came mightily upon him, and the ropes which were on his arms became as flax that has caught fire, and his bonds melted off his hands. [15]And he found a fresh jawbone of an ass, and put out his hand and seized it, and with it he slew a thousand men. [16]And Samson said,

"With the jawbone of an ass,
  heaps upon heaps,
with the jawbone of an ass
  have I slain a thousand men."

[17]When he had finished speaking, he threw away the jawbone out of his hand; and that place was called Ramathlehi.

[18]And he was very thirsty, and he called on the Lord and said, "Thou hast granted this great deliverance by the hand of thy servant; and shall I now die of thirst, and fall into the hands of the uncircumcised?" [19]And God split open the hollow place that is at Lehi, and there came water from it; and when he drank, his spirit returned, and he revived. Therefore the name of it was called Enhakkore; it is at Lehi to this day. [20]And he judged Israel in the days of the Philistines twenty years.

While there may not have been any original connection between the various stories that make up the Samson cycle except the figure of Samson himself, the editor does try to connect this chapter with the previous one by bringing in Samson's ill-fated marriage. When Samson comes to his father-in-law's home and finds that his wife is now married to another man, Samson is enraged. He avenges himself by destroying the Philistine grain crop by means of a tactic which is attested elsewhere in antiquity. Passions become further inflamed and Samson takes further action against the Philistines (vv. 6-8).

The cycle of revenge continues as the Philistines move against Judah. Evidently the tribe of Dan had already migrated to the north leaving behind some who may have engaged the Philistines through the use of guerrilla tactics and who looked for sanctuary among their fellow Israelites. The tribe of Judah is clearly reluctant to become involved in any move against the Philistines and even cooperates with them in apprehending Samson.

The force sent to Judah in order to pick up Samson was not sufficient to deal with one such as he. Samson takes up the jawbone of an ass and uses it as a weapon in making his escape from the Philistines. The jawbone was probably fashioned for use as a sickle. The use of such primitive implements was necessary because the Philistines enforced their monopoly on iron weapons and tools (1 Sam 13:19-22). While Samson could have used this primitive tool as a weapon, clearly the "thousand men" is an exaggeration. It has been suggested that the Hebrew word usually translated as "thousand" refers to the military muster of a village which would probably not exceed 20. Samson's escape would still have been spectacular.

This chapter ends with the familiar Deuteronomistic formula about the length of Samson's tenure as a judge (v. 20). This usually marks the ends of the judge's story; yet another chapter follows which brings the career of Samson to its tragic end.

The death of Samson
16:1-31

16 Samson went to Gaza, and there he saw a harlot, and he went in to her. ²The Gazites were told, "Samson has come here," and they surrounded the place and lay in wait for him all night at the gate of the city. They kept quiet all night, saying, "Let us wait till the light of the morning; then we will kill him." ³But Samson lay till midnight and at midnight he arose and took hold of the doors of the gate of the city and the two posts, and pulled them up, bar and all, and put them on his shoulders and carried them to the top of the hill that is before Hebron.

4After this he loved a woman in the valley of Sorek, whose name was Delilah. 5And the lords of the Philistines came to her and said to her, "Entice him, and see wherein his great strength lies, and by what means we may overpower him, that we may bind him to subdue him; and we will give you eleven hundred pieces of silver." 6And Delilah said to Samson, "Please tell me wherein your great strength lies, and how you might be bound, that one could subdue you." 7And Samson said to her, "If they bind me with seven fresh bowstrings which have not been dried, then I shall become weak, and be like any other man." 8Then the lords of the Philistines brought her seven fresh bowstrings which had not been dried, and she bound him with them. 9Now she had men lying in wait in an inner chamber. And she said to him, "The Philistines are upon you, Samson!" But he snapped the bowstrings, as a string of tow snaps when it touches the fire. So the secret of his strength was not known.

10And Delilah said to Samson, "Behold, you have mocked me, and told me lies; please tell me how you might be bound." 11And he said to her, "If they bind me with new ropes that have not been used, then I shall become weak, and be like any other man." 12So Delilah took new ropes and bound him with them, and said to him, "The Philistines are upon you, Samson!" And the men lying in wait were in an inner chamber. But he snapped the ropes off his arms like a thread.

13And Delilah said to Samson, "Until now you have mocked me, and told me lies; tell me how you might be bound." And he said to her, "If you weave the seven locks of my head with the web and make it tight with the pin, then I shall become weak, and be like any other man." 14So while he slept, Delilah took the seven locks of his head and wove them into the web. And she made them tight with the pin, and said to him, "The Philistines are upon you, Samson!" But he awoke from his sleep, and pulled away the pin, the loom, and the web.

¹⁵And she said to him, "How can you say, 'I love you,' when your heart is not with me? You have mocked me these three times, and you have not told me wherein your great strength lies." ¹⁶And when she pressed him hard with her words day after day, and urged him, his soul was vexed to death. ¹⁷And he told her all his mind, and said to her, "A razor has never come upon my head; for I have been a Nazirite to God from my mother's womb. If I be shaved, then my strength will leave me, and I shall become weak, and be like any other man."

¹⁸When Delilah saw that he had told her all his mind, she sent and called the lords of the Philistines, saying, "Come up this once, for he has told me all his mind." Then the lords of the Philistines came up to her, and brought the money in their hands. ¹⁹She made him sleep upon her knees; and she called a man, and had him shave off the seven locks of his head. Then she began to torment him and his strength left him. ²⁰And she said, "The Philistines are upon you, Samson!" And he awoke from his sleep, and said "I will go out as at other times, and shake myself free." And he did not know that the Lord had left him. ²¹And the Philistines seized him and gouged out his eyes, and brought him down to Gaza, and bound him with bronze fetters; and he ground at the mill in the prison. ²²But the hair of his head began to grown again after it had been shaved.

²³Now the lords of the Philistines gathered to offer a great sacrifice to Dagon their god, and to rejoice; for they said, "Our god has given Samson our enemy into our hand." ²⁴And when the people saw him, they praised their god; for they said, "Our god has given our enemy into our hand, the ravager of our country, who has slain many of us." ²⁵And when their hearts were merry, they said, "Call Samson, that he may make sport for us." So they called Samson out of the prison, and he made sport before them. They made him stand between the pillars; ²⁶and

Samson said to the lad who held him by the hand, "Let me feel the pillars on which the house rests, that I may lean against them." 27Now the house was full of men and women; all the lords of the Philistines were there, and on the roof there were about three thousand men and women, who looked on while Samson made sport.

28Then Samson called to the Lord and said, "O Lord God, remember me, I pray thee, and strengthen me, I pray thee, only this once, O God, that I may be avenged upon the Philistines for one of my two eyes." 29And Samson grasped the two middle pillars upon which the house rested, and he leaned his weight upon them, his right hand on the one and his left hand on the other. 30And Samson said, "Let me die with the Philistines." Then he bowed with all his might; and the house fell upon the lords and upon all the people that were in it. So the dead whom he slew at his death were more than those whom he had slain during his life. 31Then his brothers and all his family came down and took him and brought him up and buried him between Zorah and Eshtaol in the tomb of Manoah his father. He had judged Israel twenty years.

Samson's visit to a prostitute at Gaza provided the Philistines with an opportunity to capture him (vv. 1-3). They assumed that Samson would spend the night with the woman and consequently there was no need for immediate action. A few men could station themselves in the rooms within the city gates; these later were shut for the night. They would then be in a position to apprehend Samson the next morning. Samson foiled their plans by leaving the woman before daybreak and escaping through the gate whose doors he dismantled and carried away to Hebron. This latter feat is somewhat exaggerated to make the Philistines look rather hapless in their attempts to take Samson. The trip from Gaza to Hebron is 40 miles and it involves an ascent from sea level to 3300 feet.

Samson still has not learned how to handle himself with

women. This time he has "fallen in love" (v. 4). He naturally assumes that Delilah feels the same towards him. It is this naivete that brings Samson to his tragic end. The text does not explicitly say the Delilah is a Philistine but the implication is certainly there. She is ready to betray him without the least bit of compunction. Samson reveals the secret of his strength to Delilah since he is certain that his love would never turn against him.

Once Samson has been betrayed and caught, he is not treated like a prisoner of war or even like a slave. He becomes like a beast of burden whose sole task is to work a treadmill. What an ending this is for a judge! All this happens because Samson did not take his Nazirite vows seriously. He betrayed his vows once too often. He trusted a foreign woman once too often. Now he is abandoned by God. The exiles could have certainly recognized the history of their own nation reflected in the career of Samson, but the traditions about Samson do not end in utter defeat. Verse 22 notes that Samson's hair began to grow. For the Israelite reader this meant that the story was not over. Samson made one final, heroic and ultimately suicidal move against the Philistines. He asked for strength from God and then made an end of his tormentors. The Samson story ends with the mention of his burial and another note about the length of his judgeship (*cf.,* 15:20).

While the original stories celebrating the feat of the great Danite folk-hero Samson had little if any overt theological interest, their presence in the Book of Judges places them in a context in which theological reflection is a central purpose. The Israelite-Philistine conflict is subsumed into a more decisive conflict — the one between Israel and Yahweh. Samson's dalliance with foreign women brought him trouble, shame and finally death. Samson's neglect of his Nazirite vows eventually caught up with him. Similarly Israel's neglect of her responsibilities toward Yahweh and her dalliance with foreign powers and their divinities brought the nation trouble, shame and death. The exiles' only hope is to imitate Samson's final act of piety and pray that the Lord remember them once more (16:28).

Appendices: The Failures of the Tribes
17:1—21:25

The Book of Judges opens with the Israelite tribes doing their best to consolidate their hold on the land even though they faced serious and determined opposition from the indigenous population of Canaan. The stories from the judges describe how certain Israelite military leaders were able to unite at least some of the tribes in a common effort at dealing with the people who resisted Israel's settlement in Palestine. These efforts were at best uneven and without permanent benefit. The reason for the ultimate failure of the judges was that Israel proved to be her own worst enemy. To some extent this was dramatized through the telling of the Samson story. The last few chapters of Judges underscore these suicidal tendencies on the part of the Israelite tribes. Chapters 17-18 demonstrate Israel's self-destructiveness in the cultic sphere while chapters 19-21 deal with these same tendencies in the matter of intertribal relations.

THE SHRINE AT DAN
17:1—18:31

These two chapters tell the story of Micah and his idol which eventually is set up in a Yahwistic (!) shrine at Dan. An Ephraimite named Micah establishes a house shrine for himself. The shrine houses an image and other cultic appurtenances. Micah hires a wandering Levite originally from Bethlehem as the priest for his shrine. In the meantime, the Danites were on the move from the foothills of southwestern Palestine which they were unable to secure for themselves to a new territory far to the north near the headwaters of the Jordan River (*cf.,* Josh 19:40-48). After receiving a favorable oracle from Micah's Levite, spies from the Danites convince the rest of the tribe to carry off Micah's Levite and his shrine as well. Once the Danites acquire their own land in the north, they install the Levite and set up the cult objects in the city they renamed Dan.

The basic elements of this story reflect a period of time

when the Yahwistic cult was not bound by as many strictures as it came to be toward the end of the Biblical period. The explanation for this "laxity" is given by the editors twice in this section: there was no king in Israel at that time and people were free to do whatever they deemed to be correct (17:6; 18:1). To the exilic readers of this narrative, this explanation was highly ironic. Their experience has shown that the presence of a king on the throne of Israel does not guarantee cultic orthodoxy.

In pre-monarchic Israel then an individual might set up his own shrine to be supplied with any available personnel, though a Levitical priest was preferred. The shrine would contain certain types of equipment deemed necessary for the oracular activity that often took place there. It was a favorable oracle given to the Danite spies (18:5-6) which was seen as a sign of Yahweh's favor upon the Danites. The shrine then passed into their hands. In its original form, the story probably authenticated the Yahwistic shrine established by the Danites in their new territory. While it must be assumed that originally the establishment of the shrine at Dan was seen to be a legitimate act — in fact a response to a favorable oracle from Yahweh — the present text has turned this narrative around so that it is essentially opposed to this shrine.

The Origin of the Danite Cult Objects
17:1-6

17 There was a man of the hill country of Ephraim, whose name was Micah. ²And he said to his mother, "The eleven hundred pieces of silver which were taken from you, about which you uttered a curse, and also spoke it in my ears, behold, the silver is with me; I took it." And his mother said, "Blessed be my son by the Lord." ³And he restored the eleven hundred pieces of silver to his mother; and his mother said, "I consecrate the silver to the Lord from my hand for my son, to make a graven image and a molten image; now therefore I will restore it to you." ⁴So when he restored the money to his mother, his mother took two hundred pieces of silver, and gave it to the silversmith, who made it into a graven image and a molten image; and it was in the house of Micah. ⁵And the man Micah had a shrine, and he made an ephod and teraphim, and installed one of his sons, who became his priest. ⁶In those days there was no king in Israel; every man did what was right in his own eyes.

The name Micah begins the story with a distinct ironic twist. Here is a man whose name means "Who is like Yahweh" erecting a shrine with an image! In addition the silver which was used to fashion the image was stolen and cursed. Though the curse was removed and the silver dedicated to the Lord, only a portion of it was actually handed over for the puspose of making the sacred objects. These were the sordid beginnings of the Danite shrine.

Micah's Priest
17:7-13

⁷Now there was a young man of Bethlehem in Judah, of the family of Judah, who was a Levite; and he sojourned there. ⁸And the man departed from the town of Bethlehem in Judah, to live where he could find a place; and as he journeyed, he came to the hill country of Ephraim to the house of Micah. ⁹And Micah said to him, "From where do you come?" And he said to him, "I am a Levite of Bethlehem in Judah, and I am going to sojourn where I may find a place." ¹⁰And Micah said to him, "Stay with me, and be to me a father and a priest, and I will give you ten pieces of silver a year, and a suit of apparel, and your living." ¹¹And the Levite was content to dwell with the man; and the young man became to him like one of his sons. ¹²And Micah installed the Levite, and the young man became his priest, and was in the house of Micah. ¹³Then Micah said, "Now I know that the Lord will prosper me, because I have a Levite as priest."

At first Micah was content to have one of his own sons as the priest for his shrine (v. 6). When a Levite from Bethlehem happened to settle in Ephraim, Micah prevailed upon him to serve at his shrine. Apparently while any male Israelite could function as a priest, Levites became preferred as cultic functionaries. The text makes two rather pejorative implications about the young Levite. First, he appears as a vagabond — a wanderer who stumbles into his appointment. The second is more serious: the Levite's priesthood is bought and paid for by Micah. The Levite is not independent but is a client.

The Oracle
18:1-6

18 In those days there was no king in Israel. And in those days the tribe of the Danites was seeking for itself an inheritance to dwell in; for until then no inheritance among the tribes of Israel had fallen to them. ²So the Danites sent five able men from the whole number of their tribe, from Zorah and from Eshtaol, to spy out the land and to explore it; and they said to them, "Go and explore the land." And they came to the hill country of Ephraim, to the house of Micah, and lodged there. ³When they were by the house of Micah, they recognized the voice of the young Levite; and they turned aside and said to him, "Who brought you here? What are you doing in this place? What is your business here?" ⁴And he said to them, "Thus and thus has Micah dealt with me: he has hired me, and I have become his priest." ⁵And they said to him, "Inquire of God, we pray thee, that we may know whether the journey on which we are setting out will succeed." ⁶And the priest said to them, "Go in peace. The journey on which you go is under the eye of the Lord."

The spies from the migrating tribe of Dan pass through Ephraim on their way north. They seek an oracle at Micah's shrine. Without even employing the oracular objects found at the shrine, the Levite assures the spies of divine favor. Later this favorable oracle provides the necessary theological support for the Danites' unnecessarily violent move against the people of Laish (18:10, 27). Here is another support for a negative evaluation of the Danite shrine.

The Reconnaissance of Laish
18:7-10

> 7Then the five men departed, and came to Laish, and saw the people who were there, how they dwelt in security, after the manner of the Sidonians, quiet and unsuspecting, lacking nothing that is in the earth, and possessing wealth, and how they were far from the Sidonians and had no dealings with any one. 8And when they came to their brethren at Zorah and Eshtaol, their brethren said to them, "What do you report?" 9They said, "Arise, and let us go up against them; for we have seen the land, and behold, it is very fertile. And will you do nothing? Do not be slow to go, and enter in and possess the land. 10When you go, you will come to an unsuspecting people. The land is broad; yea, God has given it into your hands, a place where there is no lack of anything that is in the earth."

The spies come upon Laish a city which was ripe for the taking since the text implies and archaeology confirms that its defences did not include a city wall. Unlike the situation in some other Canaanite city-states, Laish was without the grave social disparity that bred the kind of tension which made revolution understandable if not inevitable. This type of social structure and the peaceful situation it engendered should have been a model for the worshippers of Yahweh rather than an object of their armed intervention.

The Theft of the Shrine
18:11-26

> 11And six hundred men of the tribe of Dan, armed with weapons of war, set forth from Zorah and Eshtaol, 12and went up and encamped at Kirjiathjearim in Judah. On this account that place is called Mahanehdan to this day;

behold, it is west of Kiriathjearim. [13]And they passed on from there to the hill country of Ephraim, and came to the house of Micah.

[14]Then the five men who had gone to spy out the country of Laish said to their brethren, "Do you know that in these houses there are an ephod, teraphim, a graven image, and a molten image? Now therefore consider what you will do." [15]And they turned aside thither, and came to the house of the young Levite, at the home of Micah, and asked him of his welfare. [16]Now the six hundred men of the Danites, armed with their weapons of war, stood by the entrance of the gate; [17]and the five men who had gone to spy out the land went up, and entered and took the graven image, the ephod, the teraphim, and the molten image, while the priest stood by the entrance of the gate with the six hundred men armed with weapons of war. [18]And when these went into Micah's house and took the graven image, the ephod, the teraphim, and the molten image, the priest said to them, "What are you doing?" [19]And they said to him, "Keep quiet, put your hand upon your mouth, and come with us, and be to us a father and a priest. Is it better for you to be priest to the house of one man, or to be priest to a tribe and family in Israel?" [20]And the priest's heart was glad; he took the ephod, and the teraphim, and the graven image, and went in the midst of the people.

[21]So they turned and departed, putting the little ones and the cattle and the goods in front of them. [22]When they were a good way from the home of Micah, the men who were in the houses near Micah's house were called out, and they overtook the Danites. [23]And they shouted to the Danites, who turned round and said to Micah, "What ails you that you come with such a company?" [24]And he said, "You take my gods which I made, and the priest, and go away, and what have I left? How then do you ask me, 'What ails you?'" [25]And the Danites said to him, "Do not let your voice be heard among us, lest angry fellows fall upon you, and you lose your life with the lives of your

household." 26Then the Danites went their way; and when Micah saw that they were too strong for him, he turned and went back to his home.

The Danites were encouraged by the favorable oracle delivered through the Levite and were intent on taking their good luck with them so they simply set about stealing Micah's cult objects and priest. The Levite is thrilled about the prospects of his new position (v. 20) and gladly cooperates in the theft of Micah's shrine. Here is another damning aspect of the origin of the Danite shrine: it was founded on a broken promise. The first chance the Levite has to move up, he abandons his former patron and seeks another more powerful one. The Levite is less free than ever before; now he is a client priest of a whole tribe.

The Shrine at Dan
18:27-31

27And taking what Micah had made, and the priest who belonged to him, the Danites came to Laish, to a people quiet and unsuspecting, and smote them with the edge of the sword, and burned the city with fire. 28And there was no deliverer because it was far from Sidon, and they had no dealings with any one. It was in the valley which belongs to Bethrehob. And they rebuilt the city, and dwelt in it. 29And they named the city Dan, after the name of Dan their ancestor, who was born to Israel; but the name of the city was Laish at the first. 30And the Danites set up the graven image for themselves; and Jonathan the son of Gershom, son of Moses, and his sons were priests to the tribe of the Danites until the day of the captivity of the land. 31So they set up Micah's graven image which he made, as long as the house of God was at Shiloh.

The key verse in this section is v. 30 which was added by the Deuteronomistic editor. It naturally raises the question: how could a shrine whose priesthood comes from Moses himself be dismantled along with the rest of what was the Northern Kingdom? The preceding sections of the narrative have provided the reasons: its cult was perverted by images; the money which established it was stolen and cursed; its priesthood, though it was descended from Moses, was venal; the city which housed it was taken by Israel in an unnecessarily violent manner. In this light the conquest of Laish is not presented as a Holy War but as a simple massacre. The fall of Dan together with its shrine, though it occurred more than 400 years later, was inevitable.

The final editors of the Deuteronomistic History saw in the ancient story of Dan's migrations and the establishment of its cultic center a paradigm of Israel's folly. The paradigm was so obvious that no explanatory digressions had to be added. The story spoke for itself. Any cult based on such foundations had to fall. Similarly no nation could expect to escape the consequences of its folly forever.

THE CIVIL WAR
19:1—21:25

The Book of Judges ends on an almost chaotic note. The tribal assembly works together for its own self-destruction. The focus of these chapters is on the civil war which threatened to eliminate the entire tribe of Benjamin (20). The story of the crime at Gibeah (19) supplies the background for the war while the final chapter (21) presents the morally outrageous attempt made by the tribes to forestall the demise of Benjamin after they did their best to accomplish just that.

The Levite and His Concubine
19:1-9

19 In those days, when there was no king in Israel, a certain Levite was sojourning in the remote parts of the hill country of Ephraim, who took to himself a concubine from Bethlehem in Judah. ²And his concubine became angry with him, and she went away from him to her father's house at Bethlehem in Judah, and was there some four months. ³Then her husband arose and went after her, to speak kindly to her and bring her back. He had with him his servant and a couple of asses. And he came to her father's house; and when the girl's father saw him, he came with joy to meet him. ⁴And his father-in-law, the girl's father, made him stay, and he remained with him three days; so they ate and drank, and lodged there. ⁵And on the fourth day they arose early in the morning, and he prepared to go; but the girl's father said to his son-in-law, "Strengthen your heart with a morsel of bread, and after that you may go." ⁶So the two men sat and ate and drank together; and the girl's father said to the man, "Be pleased to spend the night, and let your heart be merry." ⁷And when the man rose up to go, his father-in-law urged him, till he lodged there again. ⁸And on the fifth day he arose early in the morning to depart; and the girl's father said, "Strengthen your heart, and tarry until the day declines." So they ate, both of them. ⁹And when the man and his concubine and his servant rose up to depart, his father-in-law, the girl's father, said to him, "Behold, now the day has waned toward evening; pray tarry all night. Behold, the day draws to its close; lodge here and let your heart be merry; and tomorrow you shall arise early in the morning for your journey, and go home."

Apparently there were various degrees of the marital relationship in early Israel. Here the woman of Bethlehem was not the full legal wife of the Levite so the tradition simply calls her a concubine (v. 1); yet since the Levite is called her husband (v. 3), there must have been some regularity about their relationship. Though it is not crucial for an understanding of the primary thrust of the larger unit, it is important to note that the *woman* initiates the separation (v. 2) though it is sometimes assumed that only the husband had such a right (*cf.*, Deut 24:1-4). This detail prompts us to reevaluate the contemporary understanding about the status of women in ancient Israel. Apparently the woman's right to terminate a marital relationship was known.

The Gibeah Incident
19:10-30

[10]But the man would not spend the night; he rose up and departed, and arrived opposite Jebus (that is, Jerusalem). He had with him a couple of saddled asses, and his concubine was with him. [11]When they were near Jebus, the day was far spent, and the servant said to his master, "Come now, let us turn aside to this city of the Jebusites, and spend the night in it." [12]And his master said to him, "We will not turn aside into the city of foreigners, who do not belong to the people of Israel; but we will pass on to Gibeah." [13]And he said to his servant, "Come and let us draw near to one of these places, and spend the night at Gibeah or at Ramah." [14]So they passed on and went their way; and the sun went down on them near Gibeah, which belongs to Benjamin, [15]and they turned aside there, to go in and spend the night at Gibeah. And he went in and sat down in the open square of the city; for no man took them into his house to spend the night.

[16]And behold, an old man was coming from his work in the field at evening; the man was from the hill country of Ephraim, and he was sojourning in Gibeah; the men of the place were Benjaminites. [17]And he lifted up his eyes, and saw the wayfarer in the open square of the city; and the old man said, "Where are you going? and whence do you come?" [18]And he said to him, "We are passing from Bethlehem to Judah in the remote parts of the hill country of Ephraim, from which I come. I went to Bethlehem in Judah; and I am going to my home; and nobody takes me into his house. [19]We have straw and provender for our asses, with bread and wine for me and your maidservant and the young man with your servants; there is no lack of anything." [20]And the old man said, "Peace be to you; I will care for all your wants; only, do not spend the night in the square." [21]So he brought him into his house, and

gave the asses provender; and they washed their feet, and ate and drank.

[22] As they were making their hearts merry, behold, the men of the city, base fellows, beset the house round about, beating on the door; and they said to the old man, the master of the house, "Bring out the man who came into your house, that we may know him." [23] And the man, the master of the house, went out to them and said to them, "No, my brethren, do not act so wickedly; seeing that this man has come into my house, do not do this vile thing. [24] Behold, here are my virgin daughter and his concubine; let me bring them out now. Ravish them and do with them what seems good to you; but against this man do not do so vile a thing." [25] But the men would not listen to him. So the man seized his concubine, and put her out to them; and they knew her, and abused her all night until the morning. And as the dawn began to break, they let her go. [26] And as morning appeared, the woman came and fell down at the door of the man's house where her master was, till it was light.

[27] And her master rose up in the morning, and when he opened the doors of the house and went out to go on his way, behold, there was his concubine lying at the door of the house, with her hands up the threshold. [28] He said to her, "Get up, let us be going." But there was no answer. Then he put her upon the ass; and the man rose up and went away to his home. [29] And when he entered his house, he took a knife, and laying hold of his concubine he divided her, limb by limb, into twelve pieces, and sent her throughout all the territory of Israel. [30] And all who saw it said, "Such a thing has never happened or been seen from the day that the people of Israel came up out of the land of Egypt until this day; consider it, take counsel, and speak."

After the reconciliation between the Levite and his concubine, the couple travels from Bethlehem, the woman's home, back to Ephraim, the Levite's home. Rather than spend the night in a Canaanite city, the Levite prefers to travel a few more miles in order to stay in an Israelite settlement for the night. They arrive in Gibeah, which is in Benjaminite territory. They feel secure there. Though the ancient Near East is fabled for its hospitality, the people of Gibeah are uncharacteristically inhospitable. Finally a fellow Ephraimite takes in the Levite and his concubine for the night. Then the unthinkable happens. Some irresponsible men from the city ignore the sacredness of the guests within their city walls. They are ready to sexually assault the Levite. The Levite's host and the Levite himself seek to avert this outrage by suggesting another. One offers his daughter, the other his concubine to the mob. While the conduct of the mob is outrageous, the best that can be said of the Levite's is that it is cowardly and callous (vv. 26-28). The text implies that the woman died as a result of her night of horror. The Levite seeks redress of the crime committed at Gibeah by bringing the matter to the tribal authorities (vv. 29-30).

The War with Benjamin
20:1-48

20 Then all the people of Israel came out, from Dan to Beersheba, including the land of Gilead, and the congregation assembled as one man to the Lord at Mizpah. [2]And the chiefs of all the people, of all the tribes of Israel, presented themselves in the assembly of the people of God, four hundred thousand men on foot that drew the sword. [3](Now the Benjaminites heard that the people of Israel had gone up to Mizpah.) And the people of Israel said, "Tell us, how was this wickedness brought to pass?" [4]And the Levite, the husband of the woman who was murdered, answered and said, "I came to Gibeah that belongs to Benjamin, I and my concubine, to spend the night. [5]And the men of Gibeah rose against me, and beset the house round about me by night; they meant to kill me, and they ravished my concubine, and she is dead. [6]And I took my concubine and cut her in pieces, and sent her throughout all the country of the inheritance of Israel; for they have committed abomination and wantonness in Israel. ⁷Behold, you people of Israel, all of you, give your advice and counsel here."

⁸And all the people arose as one man, saying, "We will not any of us go to his tent, and none of us will return to his house. ⁹But now this is what we will do to Gibeah: we will go up against it by lot, ¹⁰and we will take ten men of a hundred throughout all the tribes of Israel, and a hundred of a thousand, and a thousand of ten thousand, to bring provisions for the people, that when they come they may requite Gibeah of Benjamin, for all the wanton crime which they have committed in Israel." ¹¹So all the men of Israel gathered against the city, united as one man.

¹²And the tribes of Israel sent men through all the tribe of Benjamin, saying, "What wickedness is this that has taken place among you? ¹³Now therefore give up the men, the base fellows in Gibeah, that we may put them to death, and put away evil from Israel." But the Benjaminites would not listen to the voice of their brethren, the people of Israel. ¹⁴And the Benjaminites came together out of the cities to Gibeah, to go out to battle against the people of Israel. ¹⁵And the Benjaminites mustered out of their cities on that day twenty-six thousand men that drew the sword, besides the inhabitants of Gibeah, who mustered seven hundred picked men. ¹⁶Among all these were seven hundred picked men who were left-handed; every one could sling a stone at a hair, and not miss. ¹⁷And the men of Israel, apart from Benjamin, mustered four hundred thousand men that drew sword; all these were men of war.

¹⁸The people of Israel arose and went up to Bethel, and inquired of God, "Which of us shall go up first to battle against the Benjaminites?" And the Lord said, "Judah shall go up first."

¹⁹Then the people of Israel rose in the morning, and encamped against Gibeah. ²⁰And the men of Israel went out to battle against Benjamin; and the men of Israel

drew up the battle line against them at Gibeah. ²¹The Benjaminites came out of Gibeah, and felled to the ground on that day twenty-two thousand of the Israelites. ²²But the people, the men of Israel, took courage, and again formed the battle line in the same place where they had formed it on the first day. ²³And the people of Israel went up and wept before the Lord until the evening; and they inquired of the Lord, "Shall we again draw near to battle against our brethren the Benjaminites?" And the Lord said, "Go up against them."

²⁴So the people of Israel came near against the Benjaminites the second day. ²⁵And Benjamin went against them out of Gibeah the second day, and felled to the ground eighteen thousand men of the people of Israel; all these were men who drew the sword. ²⁶Then all the people of Israel, the whole army, went up and came to Bethel and wept; they sat there before the Lord, and fasted that day until evening, and offered burnt offerings and peace offerings before the Lord. ²⁷And the people of Israel inquired of the Lord (for the ark of the covenant of God was there in those days, ²⁸and Phinehas the son of Eleazar, son of Aaron, ministered before it in those days), saying, "Shall we yet again go out to battle against our brethren the Benjaminites, or shall we cease?" And the Lord said, "Go up; for tomorrow I will give them into your hand."

²⁹So Israel set men in ambush round about Gibeah. ³⁰And the people of Israel went up against the Benjaminites on the third day, and set themselves in array against Gibeah, as at other times. ³¹And the Benjaminites went out against the people, and were drawn away from the city; and as at other times they began to smite and kill some of the people, in the highways, one of which goes up to Bethel and the other to Gibeah, and in the open country, about thirty men of Israel. ³²And the Benjaminites said, "They are routed before us, as at the first." But the men of Israel said, "Let us flee, and draw them away from the city to the highways." ³³And all the men of Israel

rose up out of their place, and set themselves in array at Baaltamar; and the men of Israel who were in ambush rushed out of their place west of Geba. 34 And there came against Gibeah ten thousand picked men out of all Israel, and the battle was hard; but the Benjaminites did not know that disaster was close upon them. 35 And the Lord defeated Benjamin before Israel; and the men of Israel destroyed twenty-five thousand one hundred men of Benjamin that day; all these were men who drew the sword. 36 So the Benjaminites saw that they were defeated.

The men of Israel gave ground to Benjamin, because they trusted to the men in ambush whom they had set against Gibea. 37 And the men in ambush made haste and rushed upon Gibeah; the men in ambush moved out and smote all the city with the edge of the sword. 38 Now the appointed signal between the men of Israel and the men in ambush was that when they made a great cloud of smoke rise up out of the city 39 the men of Israel should turn in battle. Now Benjamin had begun to smite and kill about thirty men of Israel; they said, "Surely they are smitten down before us, as in the first battle." 40 But when the signal began to rise out of the city in a column of smoke, the Benjaminites looked behind them; and behold, the whole of the city went up in smoke to heaven. 41 Then the men of Israel turned, and the men of Benjamin were dismayed, for they saw that disaster was close upon them. 42 Therefore they turned their backs before the men of Israel in the direction of the wilderness; but the battle overtook them, and those who came out of the cities destroyed them in the midst of them. 43 Cutting down the Benjaminites, they pursued them and trod them down from Nohah as far as opposite Gibeah on the east. 44 Eighteen thousand men of Benjamin fell, all of them men of valor. 45 And they turned and fled toward the wilderness to the rock of Rimmon; five thousand men of them were cut down in the highways, and they were pursued hard to Gidom, and two thousand men of them were slain. 46 So all who fell that day of Benjamin were twenty-five thousand men that drew the sword, all of them men of valor. [47]But six hundred men turned and fled toward the wilderness to the rock of Rimmon, and abode at the rock of Rimmon four months. [48]And the men of Israel turned back against the Benjaminites, and smote them with the sword, men and beasts and all that they found. And all the towns which they found they set on fire.

The Levite is successful in having his case heard before the intertribal authority which condemns the outrage perpetrated by the men of Gibeah. In addition positive steps are taken to punish those guilty of such an unheard of crime (vv. 1-11). The Benjaminites are requested to hand over the guilty individuals so that they may be executed (v. 12). Benjamin refuses and this is seen as an act of solidarity with the criminals. What follows is the unleashing of the tribal armies on the recalcitrant Benjaminites. At first the tribal forces experience a series of reversals (vv. 19-28), but after a carefully planned and executed ambush, the Benjaminites are thoroughly defeated with the result that only a few survivors of the tribe remained (vv. 29-48).

Certainly the impulse of the Israelite tribes to extirpate the evil committed by some of their own was perfectly understandable and was, in fact, quite expected since purging evil from Israel's midst was seen as an absolute requirement (*cf.*, Deut 13:6; 17:11; 19:13; 21:21; 22:21-22, 25; 24:7). Normally this matter should have been handled locally. The injured party's relatives should have taken care of the matter. Instead of using the normal apparatus for seeking justice, the Levite makes the affair an intertribal case. The refusal of Benjamin to hand over the criminals was less a move to protect them and more an effort to protect its own prerogatives. What made matters worse was that the intertribal assembly invokes the *herem* or Holy War, which was by this time an archaic institution, and turns it against one of its own members. As serious as the original crime was, the response was entirely out of proportion. The impression left by this entire episode is that of chaos among the tribes.

What the Canaanites were unable to accomplish, the Israelites set about doing to themselves.

Repopulating Benjamin
21:1-25

21 Now the men of Israel had sworn at Mizpah, "No one of us shall give his daughter in marriage to Benjamin." 2And the people came to Bethel, and sat there till evening before God, and they lifted up their voices and wept bitterly. 3And they said, "O Lord, the God of Israel, why has this come to pass in Israel, that there should be today one tribe lacking in Israel?" 4And on the morrow the people rose early, and built there an altar, and offered burnt offerings and peace offerings. 5And the people of Israel said, "Which of all the tribes of Israel did not come up in the assembly to the Lord?" For they had taken a great oath concerning him who did not come up to the Lord at Mizpah, saying, "He shall be put to death."6And the people of Israel had compassion for Benjamin their brother, and said, "One tribe is cut off from Israel this day. 7What shall we do for wives for those who are left, since we have sworn by the Lord that we will not give them any of our daughters for wives?"

8And they said, "What one is there of the tribes of Israel that did not come up to the Lord at Mizpah?" And behold, no one had come to the camp from Jabeshgilead, to the assembly. 9For when the people were mustered, behold, not one of the inhabitants of Jabeshgilead was there. 10So the congregation sent thither twelve thousand of their bravest men, and commanded them, "Go and smite the inhabitants of Jabeshgilead with the edge of the sword; also the women and the little ones. 11This is what you shall do; every male and every woman that has lain with a male you shall utterly destroy." 12And they found among the inhabitants of Jabeshgilead four hundred young virgins who had not known man by lying with him; and they brought them to the camp at Shiloh, which is in the land of Canaan.

¹³Then the whole congregation sent word to the Benjaminites who were at the rock of Rimmon, and proclaimed peace to them. ¹⁴And Benjamin returned at that time; and they gave them the women whom they had saved alive of the women of Jabeshgilead; but they did not suffice for them. ¹⁵And the people had compassion on Benjamin because the Lord had made a breach in the tribes of Israel.

¹⁶Then the elders of the congregation said, "What shall we do for wives for those who are left, since the women are destroyed out of Benjamin?" ¹⁷And they said, "There must be an inheritance for the survivors of Benjamin, that a tribe be not blotted out from Israel. ¹⁸Yet we cannot give them wives of our daughters." For the people of Israel had sworn, "Cursed be he who gives a wife to Benjamin." ¹⁹So they said, "Behold, there is the yearly feast of the Lord at Shiloh, which is north of Bethel, on the east of the highway that goes up from Bethel to Shechem, and south of Lebonah." ²⁰And they commanded the Benjaminites, saying, "Go and lie in wait in the vineyards, ²¹and watch; if the daughters of Shiloh come out to dance in the dances, then come out of the vineyards and seize each man his wife from the daughters of Shiloh, and go to the land of Benjamin. ²²And when their fathers or their brothers come to complain to us, we will say to them, 'Grant them graciously to us; because we did not take for each man of them his wife in battle, neither did you give them to them, else you would now be guilty.'" ²³And the Benjaminites did so, and took their wives, according to their number, from the dancers whom they carried off; then they went and returned to their inheritance, and rebuilt the towns, and dwelt in them. ²⁴And the people of Israel departed from there at that time, every man to his tribe and family, and they went out from there every man to his inheritance.

²⁵In those days there was no king in Israel; every man did what was right in his own eyes.

The final chapter of the Book of Judges intentionally portrays a pathetic picture of the Israelite tribes. Their foolish handling of the Gibeah incident, their overreaction, their massacre of Benjamin have pushed that tribe to the brink of extinction. The other tribes have to resort to murder, kidnap and rape (vv. 8-22) in order to provide the remnants of the Benjaminites with women to repopulate their tribe. These techniques are not without precedent in antiquity and they show the consequences of the folly committed in the name of just retribution.

There is no individual or group in this entire episode (except the concubine) whose conduct is not abominably immoral. The Levite and his host offer the women of their households to appease the sexual appetites of the perverts from Gibeah. The tribal assembly overreacts and forces Benjamin to take a stand which, in effect, serves to protect a mob of rapists and murderers. After the civil war is over, additional rapes and murder are necessary to restore some semblance of peace among the tribes!

The picture here is that of a sink-hole of immorality which engulfs more and more people until it almost consumes an entire tribe. Again the exilic community can recognize the morass of its own collective life — a quagmire caused by Israel and Judah's compounded infidelities. The Book of Judges ends on a tragically prophetic note. Of course, the final self-destruction of Israel was put off for a while, but it is inevitable. All that remains is for the Deuteronomist to introduce the next segment of Israel's life in her land — that of the monarchy (v. 25). What began with some promise in chapter 1 with efforts to consolidate the Israelite tribes' hold on the land ends with the chaos of a fratricidal war. Unfortunately the next segment of the story follows a similar pattern. The monarchy begins with some promise but ends destroying Israel's sacred institutions and ending her hold on the land of promise.

Conclusion

Someone once remarked that Israel's story in the Old Testament is one of unfulfilled potential. The sensitive reader is left with the impression that Israel's story just did not turn out the way it should have. This tragic element is so dominant that Judaism could not be nurtured by the Scriptures alone. There necessarily arose an entire corpus of rabbinic literature which offers the pious hope — hope based on careful observance of the Law. This tragic element in Israel's story is found already in the Books of Joshua and Judges which describe how Israel acquired the land which was promised by Yahweh.

The story begins well enough. As long as Israel followed the leadership of Joshua, she enjoyed the blessings of obedience. The armies of Israel were able to take possession of the land of Canaan by a succession of quick blows which broke the power of the Canaanite city-states and allowed the Israelite tribes to settle in the land. Joshua's farewell admonitions, however, seem to forebode a very different future for the tribes: "But just as all the good things which the Lord your God promised concerning you have been fulfilled for you, so the Lord will bring upon you all the evil things, until he have destroyed you from off this good land ...if you transgress the covenant of the Lord your God..." (Josh 23:15-16).

The Book of Judges makes it clear that shortly after the death of Joshua, the Israelites did indeed abandon Yahweh for the gods of the Canaanites (Judg 2:11-12). Fortunately for Israel God did not permit her to "perish quickly from off

210

the good land" (Josh 23:16). Though Israel had to face military threats from without, a succession of leaders emerged from the tribes. God gave these Judges victory over ancient Israel's enemies who could have dealt a fatal blow to the continued existence of the tribes in the land. Unfortunately Israel never learned from her difficult experiences with the Canaanites and repeatedly lapsed into her dalliance with the Baals. If this was not enough, the Israelite tribes began to turn against themselves. The Book of Judges ends with self-destructive chaos.

The Books of Joshua and Judges illustrate that one can never underestimate human folly. According to the presentation made by the Deuteronomists, Israel literally discarded the opportunity for a good life in a good land. But this story is not told to illustrate folly but faith. It is a testimony to the faith of Israel in Exile. Israel knew where her disobedience had brought her but she refused to accept the Exile as God's final verdict. Israel believed that God could overcome her disobedience just as easily as God overcame the armies of the Canaanites. Again and again Yahweh transformed evil into good. It is just such a God whom Israel serves — albeit feebly.

These two books are valuable precisely because of the act of faith which they exemplify. While Joshua and Judges reflect some historical data, their historical value is quite limited. The "facts" surrounding Israel's acquisition of her land serve as the backdrop for the drama of Israel's life with God. Like scenery these facts are meant to be suggestive rather than precise representations. It is a mistake to focus on the scenery when the real action takes place at center-stage — the interaction between Israel and Yahweh. The simplicity and complexity of this relationship are what occupied the narrator and should occupy the reader as well.

These books do describe how a group of tribes, united by their common worship of Yahweh, was able to acquire the land of Canaan for itself. As might be expected, there was resistance from the indigenous population of that land. At times Israel had to resort to armed conflict to overcome this resistance. At other times more peaceful means could be employed. Despite some initial success, Israel was never entirely free from pressure brought to bear by the local population. How Israel dealt with this pressure is one subject of the Books of Samuel and Kings. Now this may be a rather minimalistic assessment of the historical value of Joshua and Judges. The commentary has spoken to this issue whenever appropriate; nonetheless, it should be clear that what we call history was not a priority of the Deuteronomists.

Telling the sad and tragic story of Israel in her land as an act of faith was the sole concern of the Deuteronomists. In this story, they do not minimize Israel's sin, they do not rationalize her infidelity, they do not excuse her rebellion. It is all presented clearly, forthrightly and in stark realism. On the other hand, the story is told not for the sake of cathartic confession as if Israel's pain could be relieved by "telling all." The story is told as a bold and almost presumptive affirmation that God's act of judgment upon an unfaithful Israel is not final. It is a proclamation that human folly cannot frustrate the divine will. It is a confession which holds that God's last word to Israel will always be the same as God's first words to Abram: "...and I will bless you... and by you all the families of the earth shall bless themselves" (Gen 12:2-3).

Faith then enables believers — ancient and modern — to survive the devastating effects of sin. Though human infidelity seriously threatens our life with God, this relationship cannot be destroyed as long as an act of faith can be made even in the most feeble manner. One of ancient Israel's acts of faith in the midst of the Exile was the Deuteronomistic History of Israel in her land. This act of faith helped Israel survive the loss of her great institutions and reconstitute her life with God (*cf.*, 1 Kgs 8:46-53). How ancient Israel's life was in fact reconstituted was the accomplishment of others. The Deuteronomists simply tried to keep the embers of faith from being completely extinguished. The Synagogue and Church are living testimonies to the power of their faith.

EXCURSUS ON CHARISMATIC LEADERSHIP IN ISRAEL

The Book of Judges describes the so-called "major judges" (Judg 3:10; 4:4; 12:7; 15:20; 16:31) as military rulers who organized tribal confederations called "Israel" and went to war as the military commanders of these confederations. After achieving victory on the battlefield, these judges went on to assume the government of the tribal units which they had organized. While their office was for life, it was not hereditary although Abimelech did manage to succeed his father as ruler. His rule, however, is presented as the antithesis of that exercised by a genuine judge (Judg 9).

The government of the judges reflects the socio-political conditions of the Israelite tribes which occasionally formed confederations for the purpose of self-defense prior to the emergence of the monarchy. The questions about the judges' rule that need to be discussed here include how these judges were able to form individual tribes into leagues and what prompted the tribes to recognize and accept the authority of the judges. After all the regime of the judges does appear to be without parallel in the ancient Near East.

The Biblical narrative describes the source of the judges' power as the "spirit of the Lord" which moved the judges to act (Judg 3:10; 6:34; 11:29; 13:25; 14:6, 19; 15:14). This direct contact with divine power is recognized by the people who accept the leadership offered by the judges. This acceptance enables the judges to lead the tribes to battle and so to free the Israelites from the military and political difficulties which afflict them. While the judges' victories confirm their authority, one might ask what prompted the people to acknowledge the judges' authority *before* it is proven in battle.

It is at this point that it becomes necessary to consider the leadership provided by the judges from a socio-political perspective. Their leadership does not resemble that of the patriarchal-tribal system in which authority is diffused among a group of elders, nor does it resemble that of the monarchic system in which authority is concentrated in a bureaucratic apparatus at the head of which is the king. The rule of the judges is thoroughly personal, exclusive and independent of any hierarchic structure. This pattern of leadership has been termed "charismatic." Charismatic leaders do not owe their position to any socio-political structure but to the personal, physical and psychological attributes that set them apart from the commonplace. Ancient Israel identified the source of these attributes as the "spirit of the Lord" and so regarded the judges as divine agents with supreme authority.

The years between the first settlement of the Israelite tribes in Canaan and the establishment of the monarchy provided the situation which made the emergence of charismatic leaders a practical necessity. The Israelite tribes were involved in prolonged conflicts with the indigenous Canaanite population. Occasionally those conflicts reached critical proportions for the Israelites. The traditional forms of tribal leadership were incapable of coping with the continuing insecurity that these conflicts meant for the Israelite tribes. In these distressful times, there arose individuals whose personal initiative inspired the Israelite population, set a course of action for the people and undertook the task of eliminating the military threats posed by the Canaanites. Personal initiative by the judges followed by popular acceptance justified the description of the judges' leadership as "charismatic."

In addition to the personal initiative of the judges whose authority is then recognized by the people, there are other characteristic features of their charismatic leadership style. Since the basis of charismatic authority is *personal* endowments, the status of the judges as leaders is strictly personal and not hereditary, as has been noted above. Secondly charismatic authority is completely independent of social status, age or sex. Jephthah was a prostitute's son (Judg 11:1), Gideon was the youngest of his family (Judg 6:15) and Deborah, of course, was a woman. In addition the judges do not derive any authority from being associated with places of special status among the tribes such as Bethel, Shechem or Shiloh. Their emergence from fringe areas or insignificant places underscores the personal nature of charismatic authority. Finally charismatic authority does not depend on coercion. The judges raise armies that are composed solely of voluntary militia.

There were two principal shortcomings of the charismatic leadership provided by the judges. First no judge was ever able to unite *all* the tribes in any common effort. The largest tribal league was formed by Deborah and it contained only six tribes. Secondly the effectiveness of the judges' leadership was temporary. With the death of a particular judge, the tribes had to face a recurrence of military and political insecurity. The representatives of the tribes occasionally did try to give a more permanent form to the charismatic leadership provided by the judges (Judg 8:22). With the rise of Saul and especially David, there was an attempt to institutionalize the charisma of leadership. While the reasons for such a move are understandable, still the attempt was clearly doomed to failure.

In a certain sense, however, use of the term "charismatic" to describe the leaders of pre-monarchic Israel is a theological judgment based almost completely on the Deuteronomistic redaction of the Book of Judges. In the Deuteronomistic introduction to the book (2:6—3:6), the pre-monarchic period is described as a recurring cycle of Israel's sinning against the Lord, Israel's subjection to various Canaanite groups, and the Lord's deliverance of Israel from this subjection. This deliverance was effected through "judges" (2:16) who were raised up by the Lord and who acted under the Spirit of the Lord.

By eliminating Deuteronomistic elements from the Book of Judges we are left with a number of stories about leaders of different types who respond to different situations in different ways. They are strictly local leaders who deal with two tribes at most. (Judg 5 is the sole exception. Here six tribes are involved.) What the Deuteronomist provides is a context for these stories of famous tribal leaders of ancient times. This ambient is one of sin and deliverance. This Deuteronomistic setting transforms tribal leaders into leaders of all Israel who act under divine inspiration to deliver Israel from the effects of her sins. The model for such a portrait is probably the Deuteronomist's image of the prophets who were likewise occasional, spontaneous leaders acting under divine inspiration.

The core of the Book of Judges was a collection of stories about local leaders who exercised military command when there was an external threat to Israelite tribal life and freedom. Through a clearly discernible process of redaction the Deuteronomist portrays the Judges as "prophets" who act under the guidance of the Lord's spirit in order to deliver Israel. We owe this portrait to the Deuteronomist whose religious commitment saw all Israel's life in terms of her obedience/disobedience to the will of the Divine.

Suggestions for Further Reading

1. History of the Period

Aharoni, Y., *The Land of Israel in Biblical Times*. Philadelphia: Westminster, 1967. Replete with maps and other illustrations necessary for understanding the geographical data in Joshua and Judges.

Mazar, Benjamin, ed., *The World History of the Jewish People*. Volume III: The Judges. London: Allen, 1971. A series of historical essays by Jewish scholars. Illustrated with photographs of artifacts from the period.

Vaux, Roland de, O.P., *The Early History of Israel*. Philadelphia: Westminster, 1978. A monumental study of this period.

2. Literary analysis

Cross, Frank M., *Canaanite Myth and Hebrew Epic*. Cambridge: Harvard University Press, 1973. A series of scholarly essays. Cross suggests that there was a two-stage redaction of the Deuteronomistic History.

Noth, Martin, *The Deuteronomistic History. JSOT*, Supp., 15. Sheffield, *JSOT* Press, 1981. The essay which proposes the hypothesis of a Deuteronomistic History. A seminal work.

Polzin, Robert, *Moses and the Deuteronomist*. N.Y.: Seabury, 1980. A study of Deuteronomy, Joshua and Judges as story. A new approach to the material.

3. Sociological analysis

Gottwald, Norman K., *The Tribes of Yahweh*. Maryknoll, N.Y.: Orbis, 1979. A new and very provocative attempt to reconstruct the history of this period based in part on a Marxist philosophy of history.

4. Commentaries

Boling, Robert G. and Wright, G.E., *Joshua*. Anchor Bible, 6. Garden City, N.Y.: Doubleday, 1982.

Boling, Robert G., *Judges*. Anchor Bible, 6A. Garden City, N.Y.: Doubleday, 1975.
An excellent new translation of the text plus an illustrated commentary which reflects the perspectives of the Albright/Wright approach — especially its sensitivity to archaeological data.

Soggin, J. Alberto, *Joshua*. Old Testament Library. Philadelphia: Westminster, 1972.

——————, *Judges*. Old Testament Library. Philadelphia: Westminster, 1981.

A good supplement to Boling. Soggin's strongpoint is his concern for the history of the traditions which underlie Joshua and Judges.